TAMBOURINE:

a collection of memoir,
poetry, and fiction by
nine women authors

In Between Books

P.O. Box 790, Sausalito, CA 94966

TAMBOURINE:
a collection of memoir,
poetry, and fiction by
nine women authors

> *Karla Andersdatter*
> *CB Follett*
> *Cathy McFann*
> *Brenda McManus*
> *Sharon Savage*
> *Rosemary Sheppard*
> *Doreen Stock*
> *Christine Swanberg*
> *Sandy White*

Cover photo, typesetting, and book design
by Karla Andersdatter. The poem on the back cover
was originally published as "Healing Poem" in
The Butterfly Chronicles, 1998. Photo and original
painting p.1, by Karla Andersdatter, photo p.105 by Doreen
Stock, photo and original painting p, 11 by Sandy White,
original painting p.90 by CB Follett, photo of painting p.90
by Jeremy Thornton, photo p. 23 by Jeff Swanberg

Published by In Between Books Publishing Co.,
a subdivision of the House at the Butterfly Tree,
P.O. Box 790, Sausalito, CA 94966

Library of Congress Preassigned Card Numnber: 00-104971
ISBN 0935430121

Printed in the United States of America, September, 2000

TABLE OF CONTENTS

Seventeen
and Thirty-One

Cathy McFann

CATHY McFANN

If destiny comes to help you,
Love will come to meet you.
A life without love is not a life.
    Rumi

This story was written in my thirty-first year. It is a reflection of memory. I was seventeen in 1970. Times were changing. My high school years were spent in a small town in the central coast of California. Now, at forty-eight (17+31), I live in Sonoma County, north of San Francisco. I live in a house in a garden with my son, Ben, and my husband Paul, two cats, thirteen doves, a gold fish and a hermit crab.

I had not written much for several years. I asked for inner guidance about what to do now, at this particular moment in my life. Karla called and asked if I would like to publish this story. I think it is time to begin writing again.

I find both love and writing disrupt, embarrass, and unsettle my life. I am grateful for all the many forms and ways in which love has entered my life.

SEVENTEEN AND THIRTY-ONE

"She lay on the bed. He was in the kitchen. She could hear him talking, laughing with his friend. He sounded drunk. He <u>was</u> drunk. She turned over and wondered how she could get through the kitchen to the other bedroom where her clothes lay heaped upon the floor. She was drunk too. Maybe it would be easier just to walk through the kitchen and pretend that she was not ashamed.

It was not quite the romance of the first night. Then they had been very much alone and very drunk. But the wine had not made the magic. It had been the long wait and the forbiddenness of the act. (She was seventeen. He was thirty-one. She was his student. He was her English teacher.) They had made love. They fucked. They did both. It was under the stars. She remembered the sky. Orion was in the sky."

That's how I would begin the story. A little cheap and romantic. You see I was the girl and you were the man. It is our story and in writing it I remember what it was like to be seventeen and very much in love, aware of being so. Writing this you are still in mind. You cause me to wonder if my sentences make sense, if they are structured to read well or whether you would red pencil them. I have imagined writing you this story because you were the one person who took my writing seriously. But I have also imagined writing you this story to make you take seriously what you left so undone.

But at some point I must have known . . . known what? At some point it began to occur to me. I remember coming out to your house. You had been drinking, drinking in the summer sun by the algae green pool, discussing probably, existential heroes, and whose ass had what shape. It was late afternoon and I was very sober. You started to tell me about trimming the apple tree and how a girl had helped you hold the ladder. You told me the story once before but she was me and I held the ladder and you had forgotten.

You were of course very honest. You slept with many women. You told me so. Probably not as many as you would have had me imagine. That was part of your story. But this is not your story. It is mine. I don't remember the beginning. The sequence seems confused. It was years ago. I dreamed about you for years.

I guess it began in writing. It was the journal that let you see inside me. You took me seriously. I took myself seriously. I wrote sensitive poetry. I sat and watched the Christ statue in the Mission courtyard and wondered if it did or really could move. If anyone should have asked, of course, I knew it was of plaster. I veiled the edges of my uncertainty in poetic color. I was hungry for magic, for magic and meaning. I was seventeen. I began to write for you. It was an assignment but I wanted you to know me, so I told you secrets and hinted at how much I saw and how much I knew. I always hinted and was never direct because there were many things I did not know.

Or maybe it began when you would come into your Literature of Alienation Class and drink mayonnaise jars full of water. Always on Mondays you drank lots of water and you talked of Sarte and Camus.

You were not that handsome. I remember your fingers were

4

almost short, but somehow they were also delicate. (Perhaps that is my romance, to think that they were delicate.) I think that they were short and I always feel tender when I remember them. Once you were filing your nails in class. You were talking and laughing. Someone else was there. He thought it strange that a man would file his fingernails in public. You were vain. You were very vain. You were also sexy in your tight Italian pants, high waisted and cut close. You never wore underwear. And your shirts were always white. The fabric was close to your skin and I wanted to know how it felt. Was it like silk? Maybe they were polyester or maybe cotton but they were always open at the neck. Your clothes always reminded me that you had been a barker on North Beach. Not really a barker. You were a tour guide for a bus company. I can't remember exactly. But your shirts and the way that your chest was so close to the fabric made me want to touch you.

You read what I wrote and you made me rewrite it. You were my high school teacher. I was in love with you, or I was coming to be in love with you. You invited me after class to go to breakfast with you. You were taking a chance. I was charmed and impressed.

We had breakfast downtown, at an outdoor cafe. Sometimes, I remember and can imagine how the scene would fit into the story. It would be near the beginning.

"As a couple they were not extraordinary. He was older. He talked and for the most part she listened. It was obvious if anyone had cared to notice that she was very much taken with him.. She was in love with him, but her reserve was such that it was only in watching and noticing the softness in her hands reaching for the water glass, the way her fingers reached and felt the moist coolness, as she looked at him, it was obvious in that way that she longed to touch him. He did not seem so in love. He enjoyed being with her, flirting and telling her stories. She smiled, embarrassed. They didn't seem intimate enough to be lovers but from watching, one might suspect that was his intention. And if one was just a bit

more observant, perhaps someone who watched from the table in the corner, might have noted in the way his eyes followed the curve of her shoulder to the soft hollow, that such fantasies were definitely on his mind and that he would like to touch her.

"I am looking for the answer or at least a partial answer to loneliness. Perhaps it is somewhere near love, somewhere near trusting; giving and receiving without fear."

(Right now, I want to remind you that I was seventeen. Because again I feel naked and young and I want to protect her, that young girl of my features. How could I have been so honest? I was speaking to you. I wanted you to love me.)

You answered: "Love" (you do not write this word, but circle it from my context) "is to stop fearing and means you are not all you can know (or need) of the universe."

We went to Tassajara together. It was a Zen Center. A place of meditation and retreat. In so much quietude you seemed very much out of place. You wanted to fuck in the river but the water was too cold. I wonder now why you wanted to go to a Zen center. Was I a soul image for you. . . quiet, poetic? You were certainly lonely, too troubled to be in harmony with the hot summer valley and meditating monks. You always imagined that god's face was half turned from you. You would never see his face. You were young and indolent, irreverent and often drunk. Your heroes were the Ginger Man and Zorba. What were we doing in a Zen Center?

I wrote poems for the high school journal. Some of them were for you. No one else knew. I think even you did not know how many of my poems were for you. I wrote: *"A fine thin coat/ you wrapped down/ upon my trembling shoulders/To ward and warm/ the empty night./ Now though the warp of slender promise/ so hard to trade a fine thin coat/ for colors of a new day."*

You were an obsession for many years. I held part of myself in reserve. It stayed dreaming with you. Nothing could quite compare with what was unlived. So I stayed wistful for an adolescence, when hope was something I could live on. I stayed dreaming of you and other ends to our romance but needing also the bittersweet of the story to sustain me. I dreamt about you for years, not often, but you always seemed a real presence. I missed you. I never told anyone how important you were. I was embarrassed by my love, embarrassed and nearly ashamed, that anyone should ever see me again— naked, and uncovered in longing for you.

But back to the story. It really is a love story. At seventeen, I could not say that very simply. I didn't understand how it could be a true story without the mystery and the intrigue, without the hiding and the veiling. I was in love with you.

Lying with you that night, I was happy. For a little while, I felt warm and real. You fell asleep. I was awake. It was summer and we were on the patio. It was enclosed, so no one could see us lying together. Our lovemaking was one of those moments I always doubt in retrospect, because to say that the sky opened and for some moments I was lost in being touched by you, is to be naked again to being seventeen and being myself. But it was true and since this story is for you, I am not so embarrassed. It was a rare moment. I wrote then in my own journal, the one I did not show to anyone: *"Your body is a landscape, a seascape, a sunscape changing in reflection, changing with the distance and the day. To know, the artist sees with brush and crimson sun. To know, I touch in faulty gesture, the river and the sunglade of your flesh. As I lie with you I wonder how long to know your body. I do not even question time to know such strange smiles."*

The last line of the poem was a seduction. It was also true. It added just that slightly fey quality that made me, I believed, somehow appealing. I did give you that poem, later. . . When was it? I don't remember. Sometime after the summer we made love. But I never gave you this next poem:

> *"I could not sleep last night*
> *I could not read last night*
> *I could not write last night*
> *I could not anything last night,*
> *because of you. . .*

I am afraid that I love you.
Tonight as I lie alone
I am afraid that I love you."

And now, for a moment it is difficult to continue the story. Because I know it ended? Because the next part has less romance and is more painful? Because for years I've thought about this story? I have wondered if I could write it if you did not love me. I am writing this story and I did love you and I do not know if you loved me.

I was seventeen. I was reading the <u>Feminine Mystique</u> and <u>The Second Sex</u>. I asked you to help me with an independent tutorial on the "Feminine Identity".

I was trying to understand who I was. You were very much involved in that definition. I wanted to know who I was as a woman. I was trying to name the subjectivity of myself. There was little history, little literature to which I could refer. The women's movement had just begun. I was just becoming a woman. I wanted you to know me. I did not know myself.

Do you remember that Simone DeBeauvoir said in the <u>Second Sex</u>, "*When man makes woman the Other, he may then, expect her to manifest deep seated tendencies toward complicity. Thus woman may fail to lay claim to her status as subject because she lacks the definite resources, because she feels the necessary bond that ties her to man regardless of reciprocity, and because she often is pleased with her role as the Other.*"

Can you image how it was then? I covered the <u>Second Sex</u> with a plain brown book cover. There was a picture of a nude woman on the front cover. I was embarrassed to have the cover seen. It was easier just to hide the picture. Remember I was seventeen.

We argued some, in this independent study. But mostly, I remained hesitant, hidden, careful not to offend. I remained enveloped in the feminine mystique. I wanted you to love me. You were never more seductive. As I would begin to speak, you would admire me, you would watch the way I moved. I forgot my words and was turned back, my body the focus of attention. I needed to talk to you but I also wanted you to desire me, because I desired you or myself or some reflection I found in your eyes. As I spoke you watched and I found myself filled with an awareness of being a woman, not quite myself but someone desirable.

How fumbling and inarticulate I must have sounded. I borrowed words from Simone DeBeauvoir. I tried to explain that the Other was not who I knew myself to be. But you could not help me. You were too busy seducing me and protecting yourself, turning my focus through your gaze, back upon myself. I always felt that I was blushing as I talked, as I tried to let you and myself understand just how this feminine mystique was a veiling that shadowed my words.

If I had pushed against the shaping of your vision, I was in danger of losing you. So I stayed within the reflection of my form. I did not want to frighten you away. So I gave up listening to my own voice. Over the years, those first hesitant words grew dusty and forgotten. The poems remained precious and undeveloped. I kept them hidden so that I would remain always seventeen and you might love me. Yet my bookshelves filled with the words of other women, and these words echoed the unspoken phrases of myself. Through their visions the world began to take shape before my eyes. I listened for a long time before I knew that this story was mine.

How did the story end? With your telling me that you would be living with another woman? With your telling me that it would be best for us to no longer see each other? How did it end? Did it end the night I drove home and realized you drank too much? Or was it the next day when I met another a man? Was it over then?

Did it end when I left school a semester early? Or maybe it continued on into that second summer. Your new lover had left and my new lover had not lived up to your image. You and I saw each other once, maybe twice that summer.

Or maybe it ended when you called me and you were lonely. I could hear that you might need me and I was frightened by that need. When I left for college, it should have been over. But you came once to visit me. I wasn't home. The second or third Christmas card could have been the last. You always included a note. It grew less familiar over the years but you always sent a card.

When I heard that you got married, I took a long walk in the hills. I had dreamed of you the week before, of you and another woman. I wrote you a short letter - congratulations and goodbye. You responded with a note.

And still sometimes, I wished my lover were you.

Last year you wrote me a letter. It was something of a confession and something of an apology. I cried when I read it. You wished me well in my marriage, and told me you were happy in yours. You told me in your letter that you hoped I was still writing. You told me my writing was good and that reading it years later, you had begun to understand.

This story ends in writing. That's how it began. You were my first love. You were my first critic. You were my teacher. I wrote for you. You were thirty-one and I was seventeen. When you rejected me I believed you. I trusted your judgement. I continued to love you, for years I continued to love you.

When I began to write again, this story seemed too subjective, too true. I wanted to write of some event abstracted and reformed so that it was not so intimately connected with the threads of my own life. But that seems partly the point that this story is coming to.

I wanted you to know how I had lived this story. It is true. It is not a fiction. I was seventeen and you were thirty-one. Now I am thirty-one and can remember seventeen. You see, I could have found a metaphor, but this one just happens to be true.

The Lady Who
Sawed Herself in Two

Sandy White

SANDY WHITE

"I grew up in the southeastern hills of Pennsylvania, eventually moving to Delaware as the sixties came upon my teenage years. I had known, from an early childhood filled with no friends to talk with but the breezes and the critters, that I could distill language into poetry and visions into paint, and sound into music. The first organized pursuit was obtaining a degree in fine arts with a major in painting, leaving home at age 16 to accomplish this. Eventually landing in California on a series of sinking houseboats, poetry showed up again when pen and paper replaced oil painting, due to the sawdust from construction. I discovered what I already knew, that artistic discernment traveled from one medium to another. Writing during this time had much to do with the aching that accompanied the strain of listening for something to break through into emptiness, and how I could get empty enough to hear it better."

Sandy White lives with her son Nick in Woodacre, CA.

LEFTOVER WOOD

The leftover wood
from the house
you built

kept me warm
all winter long
even if

you didn't.

My springtime love
is heartily chopping up
the rest.

He doesn't know
it came from your house.
He has never
heard about you.

I like to listen to him
whistle and wield
the hatchet.

I like to watch
him make your wood
disappear.

He thinks I am smiling
because I am pleased.

THE DECEPTION

They deceived each other.
Neither knew how it started, yet
it existed between them.

One day, the lie became too thin.
Transparencies hung about in the air
and draped around the necks
of those who came to visit.

A band of angels danced through
in an effort to filter the room, but
could not persuade the lie to stop.

The visitors, at first
did not recognize the lie.
The band of angels, good at exposing
such matters, succeeded, and that day
after the visitors departed, both
realized they no longer needed
to pretend
and the rawness of truth fell
upon them, as only
the rawness of truth can.

Layer after layer after layer
peeled back, until neither knew
if either could ever be connected
to a center ever again, when
the most monumental of all truths
revealed itself: they had needed their lie
as life itself
needed breath.

The band of angels, their devilish
work done, restored the bond
between them
and flew away . . . after all
they were only apprentices.

And the two continued to deceive
one another, but this time

they knew what they were doing.

THE LADY WHO SAWED
HERSELF IN TWO

because nobody else would.

She longed for one
man to divide her.

Yet among hypnotists
charmers, tricksters, even
the stongest of magicians
no one knew powers
of completion, of opposite.
There was no half or other
among the fireball eaters
escape artists or sword swallowers.

So with her own sleight hand
she fastened stiffly to her upper lip
a villainous mustache. Then
like Little Nell, upon a log, in an
old sawmill, she laid herself down
and the buzz saw severed her half
that was fast to the eye of the moon
from the half that was not.

From handkerchiefs of fluttering silk
she emerged, as a pair of white doves
without a cage. Star of her own
balancing show, she went on to become
her own yin, her own yang
pulling her selves like rabbits
out of a hat.

MUCH AS MEN DO

Mother went to war when she cleaned
battling against a world returning
to dust, ever falling apart
with an army of detergent
an arsenal of broom and mop

nothing stopped her.

That old war horse, the Hoover
trooped over floor boards through
my Saturday morning cartoons, while
mother sang, "Onward Christian Soldiers".
Dissolvers of dirt obsessed her, as did
strategies, chemicals, and each new
final solution to eradicate the enemy

much as men do when
men go to war

embracing the thrill of the hunt.
Mother fought to maintain certain
qualities of existence. Spiders, dust
bunnies, balls of grease, met their ends
exterminated in the incinerator
as carcasses, as burning cadavers

much as men do when
men go to war.

REMINISCING

Remember the night
you were the Big Dipper
and I was a galaxy, when all
the stars exploding, poured
down from the Milky Way
right into my throat?

Or remember that time
our bed turned
into an Indian blanket?
Beneath buffalo robes
we both knew it was snowing
even though it was summer.

And when the room shifted
into bamboo! You
were the moon
blooming over an ocean
and I, a white flower
in your mouth.

STAG IN THE FOREST

antler moss scarred velvet
branched crown heavy
shoulders soft fur
moist nostril, acquiver

wild light, eyes breathe mist
into mine, my trunk in
dizziness, my limbs, arms
fallen, not unlike leaves
vines, loglike legs, boughed
nerves crackling brush
crunched under mounting
hoof, trickling sprung from
swollen thicket thighs, my verdant

mind swirling, winding out
star-studded in a blackened sky, I
am not . . . this time . . your doe
we meet this time
and I am the whole forest

KISS

Gather
my wrists
and smother
once and for all
for all time, these
pale edges, this
open seam
these lips, this strip
of a smile.

Fasten
your lips
preciously and seal
my mouth, this wound
this quivering
cave with your
rock, your flesh
of stone, until I
am healed by
your kiss.

Cure
the gaping dream
the grand craving.
Mend
a lifelong sorrow.
O give

me your kiss
your bandage
your tourniquet.

TRAIN RIDE

This morning I was a tunnel
in the side of a mountain
and you, were an engine
at the head of a train

making sounds a train makes
as it moves through
a sleepy southern town
rolling with the

rhythm of a
train's wheels.
When you came to the other
side of the tunnel

the train stopped
and let out all your sperm.
They were wearing top hats
three piece suits

and carrying canes.
Parasols flourished
as did petticoats and flounces
of ruffled lace.

They all promenaded
ever so slowly, chatting
about the truly fine
morning it was.

CERTAIN MEN CAN'T TALK
ABOUT THE MOON

Month after month, lifting petticoats to the moon
with a man, softly, in the night shadows
to his whim, whispering not a single word, not
even one (I know my visitor is fragile).
But the moon raged too beautifully. Thoughts
swelled like oceans behind my lips.
The sacred silence burst when I spoke and words
fell like rocks, like rocks from my mouth.

Certain men can't talk about the moon anymore.
It reminds them of something to evade, something
dangerous or sticky. Their necks begin to strain
and itch uneasily, embarrassed as plumbers whose
pipes have sprung a leak. Circuits inside their
brains shut down faster than lightning bolts.
Old schedules of trains fall suddenly from pockets.
Windows suggest memories of fresher, less
resounding air. They are terrified someone can hear
their hearts breathe again, that someone might
set her clock by it.

Such alchemists, these men, who tip-toe in and out
with the moon. You know the kind. They're tough.
They work with wheels and pulleys and switches
taming machines, competing for record time.
Jousting for power with one another. They make
matter whirr and buzz and whiz. Their souls
embrace tools, things they can touch and measure.
Their fingers caress oiled metal gently
like rose petals. It's times like these
I wish I'd never seen a moon.
It's times like these I wish I were a carburetor.

The Wide Wisconsin Prairie

Christine Swanberg

CHRISTINE SWANBERG

"My beginnings were humble. The first five years of my life were in a small cottage on Lake Lorraine in Whitewater, Wisconsin. I had no playmates except animals and the lake. I think these beginnings are part of the reason I am drawn to and practice a somewhat simple and monastic life in which solitude, animals, and garden play a big part. Perhaps I spent thirty years of working a dynamic teaching career with the goal of returning to this still point. I was raised in the 50's, a superficial time of poodle skirts and rock and roll, yet under the surface a revolution stirred. I became an English teacher, mentoring young writers, at a large city high school. The more I taught creative writing, the less I wanted to teach it—and the more I wanted to write. I took a couple of sabbaticals to work with a number of great American writers, in particular, Lucien Stryk and Lynda Hull. I worked passionately and persistently until writing poetry became a Zen focus. Though I experiment with other genre, I always return to poetry. Perhaps because it embraces all the best of me: mystic, lover, friend, adventurer, story teller, musician, actress, and healer. For me, it is the most satisfying and comprehensively expressive art . At its best it can be a healing incantation. Poetry is the place where I discover what I truly am, deep at the still core."

Ms. Swanberg has produced six collections of poetry: Tonight on This Late Road, Invisible String, Bread Upon the Waters, Slow Miracle, The Tenderness of Memory, and Where the Enchanted Live. Recently, her poetry won first place in Poet's West and the Hal Grutzmacher Award for Poetry.

Grateful acknowledgement is given to the editors of journals in which these poems first appeared: "Wide Wisconsin Prairie" in Sow's Ear and Poet's West, "The Red Laquer Room" in The Butterfly Chronicles, Prairie Winds, Rock River Times, and Poet's West, "Dream Catcher" in The Butterfly Chronicles, "The Rings of Saturn" in Prairie Winds and Poet's West.

THE WIDE WISCONSIN PRAIRIE

We were walking in the wide Wisconsin prairie
before you mounted
the gleaming black motorcycle,

kicked it into gear and left me

for good, there in the goldenrod and
wood lilies that too hot October day
beneath an overzealous sun

for good.

I knelt in prairie grass, bending
in your leaving like the long clumps of asters
and windblown tassels;

that scorched indian summer

before a terrifying sun that
burned the glacial moor.

Think of me as one who begs
just once, then gives her grief
to the sweet black earth that cradles

November. Think of me as a fallow field where red-
hawks glide. Think of me as one who burns the
prairie like a Chippewa whose courage is
wide and slow and complete.

THE RED LAQUER ROOM
for Linda Hull

We were hiding in the Red Laquer Room,
the empty dance floor of the grand old
      Palmer House.
Deep in the center of Chicago, its black canyons,
dark skyscrapers, faint friction and sparks
of the El clamoring like a craving. You said
I'd be surprised how you'd lost your beauty.

Thin as a refugee, your black and blue babushka
      twirled
into a turban high Bohemian style, you seemed
more like some ragged survivor than the gypsy
that you were. Dear Lynda, even when we dared
flick on the great white chandeliers
in the Red Laquer Room, I knew the streets

had won, but pretended we crouched together
in a lovely surreal dream where happy endings
bright as crystal chandeliers in ballrooms still
      glow.
I thought surely you'd find a way past
the city's chaos, jagged graffiti, pain of cracked
pavements, heels crushing, the stone souls.

I thought you might find stillness in the lake's
lapping tongues, a lilting gull, some small place
not quite ecstasy. But no, you could never
be consoled by compromise, or live slowly
to earn an ending less violent, never fail to see
the teeth behind the tongue.

Today I entered a store with delicious and sad
surprises—red laquer boxes
where gypsies and czarinas dance in snow and fine
horses with arched necks bow their heads.
I hold this red laquer bowl, deep wooden spoon,
remember how you fed me with poems as fine
as this red glossy wood. I recall

a recurring dream that finally came true:
I walked in the white arctic night
beneath the swirls of Saint Basil's,
heels gliding over the bricks of Red Square.
At that moment I lost a world that cannot be
measured in square feet. You were there too.

WINTER MOOD

Sometimes winter shocks us
with its vim and happy
mittens, red, endless
crafts, cookies, lines,
a streudel of busyness.

We the winter blue
find the frenzy way too green
with money and dyed pine,
hear instead a solo Celtic harp
near midnight Venus and the moon,

find the season winter
erotic, melancholy, Baby,
like the muffled bird cry
past an icy feathered attic window,
clutching panes like the love

we long for past all reason.
Or desire that hangs like mistletoe
above the door where
wishes don't come true, and
the ice in your chest never melts.

DREAM CATCHER

floats

above the weathered, wooden window
in the attic where I sleep under white
satin comforter, moon streaming through
the skylight bright winter nights,

holds

a needle pulled from my tongue
in last night's dream, a talking needle
that travelled through my veins
slipped through my heart,
stuck in my tongue.

The dream catcher adds it to our
web of dreams: a shard of glass
that cut my lip,
a butterfly on the nose of the horse
I once owned, an archangel on my porch,
a cathedral where I fly
singing like Kathleen Battle.

Last night
the Dream Catcher Herself came to me,

says she wants Overtime
for work far beyond the call of duty:
an ocean storm turning the soft sky black,
the golden ferret snoring behind the sofa,
all the blue and orange Persian kittens.

She pets a white llama alone in a corral
where the landscape makes no sense,
talks back to the needle who speaks
a hard alien tongue.

SUPPOSE WINTER

Suppose winter were license
to be like trees and bears,
a simple barren time of sleep and fur,
snoring and huddling,
the drawing of deep cold water
from black root and river bottom,
the best long rest by fire, brightest
January sun through bare branches.

Suppose winter were a drug,
splash of morphine on the rocks,
and the simplest chores, say
polishing silver spoons shows you
the lost art of embossing:
a sheaf of wheat on a curved handle,
a thumbnail bear, MISSOURI. (Do people
really live there? Do they love company?)

Suppose the winter wind that scalps
the leafless Norway maple and makes
the weeping willow brush the river's icy
edge has nothing to do with you
hibernating in the blue comforter
awakened only by the lover you haven't named,
your invisible winter lover, dream
of climax unexpected and complete.

Suppose winter were a white wolf
resurrected, a howl within your ribs
that longs for icy solitiude, that place
where all the pleasant masks are hung
to dry beside red, wet parkas,
the cheery nubby mittens, the closet
where the one ferocious muse
finally has her way with you.

THE RINGS OF SATURN

"Saturn is the planet of responsibility
and symbolizes the ethic of hard work.
Under its influence a person's character
is strengthened through trial and difficulty."
                    Joanna Woolfolk

After seeing the rings of Saturn through binoculars
from a balmy bluff in indian summer,
in the Milky Way's vast sweep of stars and nebulae,
the dusky dome where no city lights intrude,

after dreaming that we skated on the rings
of Saturn, red and black ice,
the celestial overpass, where no one honks,
that unencumbered silence, it is enough

to wake blue and ornery,
forget our daily affirmations,
have a second cup of hot black coffee
out of the old wheelthrown, ringed mug

now chipped at the lip. Still
it's speckled like the firmament
and the coffee's good. Our daily fire.
It is enough to iron in the cold basement,

spray startch on cotton, glide
through domestic wrinkles, your bleached
white shirt which I prepare for you,   ·
like bread, over and over.

It is enough to fold white underwear,
warm and soft as dough, this private ritual grown
through a quarter century of better-or-worse.
It is enough to find a lady bug

on the old wooden headboard
of the waterbed we refuse to give up
and leave her there for luck. Well,
it's mostly better, isn't it?

We grow old skating under Saturn,
making the most out of our blue, imperfect
planet, our blue, imperfcct lives,
dismantling and remantling our dreams.

Voyagers 1 & 2. We distill, ironing
and pruning and changing our plans.
Yet in these rings of years, we keep the fire
of a life imagined well. The future swells

like steam from coffee mugs,
the lady bug flies, and our handmade
wedding bands with gold and silver strata
carve their callous rings around our fingers.

WHIPPOORWILL

If love were a whippoorwill, he would fly
to me in indian summer. We'd spiral

high against the golden autumn sky,
dive for last dreamy, dusky-winged moths,

loop around poplar tops over and over
until we'd have our fill. I'd accept

dark chimneys of sleep, the sacred soot
and smoke, cool dormancy we must keep

in order to endure. We'd take each day,
every harbored snowfall. Who knows why

some hearts open again like the dwarf red rose,
tender perennial, or why some cease for keeps.

Where does he vanish, the whippoorwill who
does not come again, his forlorn call?

Last night I dreamed he wrapped me
in his wings. We were quiet long and then

he sang his wild summer song. We sailed above
the scraggy trees, chased the sun that set behind

long, black chimneys. When the furious breeze
allowed, we arced between the moon and Venus.

We survived, didn't we. . . you and I, when clouds
like whippoorwills' wings wisp across the sky.

RETIREMENT

I love the Zen of it:
      contentment in cleaning a closet,
      satin-finished joy of painting a door,
      green pleasure of singing Evensong,
      deep spell of reading hardbound library
          books,
      sheer greed of writing poetry on call.

I love the slow graceful pace:
      tinkering with tarnished brass
      painting an archway periwinkle
      sorting out clothes I'll never need to wear
      wearing only comfortable cottons
      planning a trip without mania.

I love the way I begin to flow:
      meandering through rooms with new eyes
      converging at a desk where stacked books
          beckon
      like fresh coffee, my morning's
          transfusion
      crashing on the telemarketer who disrupts
          my reverie
      freezing with all the *no's* that hitherto
          were not.

I love loosening *'nots'* of worry:
    sleep's not an acrobat turning cartwheels
    morning's not a gaggle of pantyhose with
        holes
    lunch is not a microwave within
        stale, stifled walls
    afternoon's not a cardboard office
    evening's not collapse time in front of
        reruns.

I dig reaping renegade seeds:
    patience to listen to an ancient aunt
    delicious interest of wise investment
    sweet voice reaching a four octave range
    kooky, bad novella finished and shelved
    speaking Italian pui bene. Si? Bellisima?

I love the way one thing leads to another:
    a nudge becomes a poem
    a phone call becomes a scheme
    a color becomes a new room
    a spice becomes a feast
    a book— an odyssey.

Holding On To It

Brenda McManus

BRENDA McMANUS

"Born in 1940 in the little town of Horwich at the foot of the Moors and the Pennines, I was a child of the war but not directly in it. Hitler's bombs didn't find us but nevertheless my mother placed me in a washing basket and into the shelters we'd go every time she heard a bomber going to its mark in London.

The derivation of the name Horwich means a family community which has settled on higher ground, and this small town has many hills and dales leading to lovely walks in the country. Horwich, set in the county of Lancashire, is a place of moors and mists, castles on hills, stone walls, lakes, heather and sheep, of cotton mills and clogs, fairies, hobbits and witches, splendid rivers, and a medieval history going back before 1588, including both Roman and Norman conquests. A copious supply of coal and water changed Lancashire from a farming to an industrial society when weaving cotton and textiles became a supportive industry.

My family worked in the cotton mills. My mother and my Scots grandma weaving towels whilst my uncle was a foreman in the weaving sheds. I was a creeler, someone who keeps all the bobbins full on the loom for the weaver. I did this for two years before coming to America at seventeen.

I have always been a fervent reader, feeling my way through stories as if to name and make sense of my life and times. I have enjoyed a tremendous amount of healing with writing as my tool. I will be 60 this year, and find a growing need to set down in pen and ink, the written word of my past, so my children and grandchildren will know who they are."

Ms. McManus has had articles published in *Pacific Sun, The Bernal Journal*, and *The Butterfly Chronicles*. "Harvey Milk" was first published in the *Noe Valley Voice*. "Husbandry" was first published in MALT {Marin Agricultural Land Trust}*Magazine*.

NEMAST'E

On the beach I watch two young girls wearing gauzy pale colored dresses. I'm sitting with my back pressed to a rock watching the ocean— and them. One of them has rolled up her skirt between her legs and tucked it in the waist band of her skirt Now, arms held up to the sky, they are doing salutations to the sun. Dancing in and out of the water, they push a stick into the sand and clasping hands, sing and chant around it, laughing, giggling. A ceremony to the penis maybe, a fertility rite, a witches' song, a young girls' desires?

I've felt barren lately, dumb and sluggish in my head. I want to go to bed with good books for as long as it takes me to stir and re-vitalize. I feel like leaf mould, compost in fermentation time. The yeast of my spirit is percolating in the cauldron.

There is a saying that the first four letters of Buddha means to be awake. I do not want to be awake. I want to be asleep and in my subconscious; to wake, drink tea, and read another book till I slip back into the darkness. It's all I want to do. At the gas station, there is a man whose hands are sharply bent at the wrists where his jacket sleeves end, so distorted that at first I mistakenly thought he had no hands. What I was seeing was the knobs of his wrists at the mid-carpal joints. his finger-tips clawed and frozen, almost touching the inside veins of his wrists. When he asked me if he could pump gas for me I said yes, wondering how he was going to manage to do that. I asked him what happened to his hands and he showed me and said, "I was born like that ma'am."

Crossing the street in San Francisco a young woman of medium height, light brown skin, round voluptuous body, wearing a golden brown curly wig and a long raincoat, walks across the street between 17th and Folsom, where I'm sitting in my car waiting for a green light. Gesturing with two fingers stabbing repeatedly in the air she makes fuck you motions. Jabbering away in a loud voice, she suddenly stops and hoists up the back of the raincoat to reveal panties and tights rolled down under her bare butt. Not for one second breaking stride she reaches back with both hands, bends forward at the waist and spreads her cheeks as if to say, I shit on you, world.

In the darkness of the night the soft blurry ring of light around the moon beckons me, imprinting an aching pattern on my heart. The fragrance of huge white blossoms in the tree close by fills my body.

I think of Mimi, my nine-year-old next door neighbor.

"Hi, can I come in?" she had called at eight thirty this morning. "Let's close the curtains and streak". Her blonde spontaneity bubbled in the air.

I take Robert, my ebullient two-year-old grandson, to the kids' playground. In a quiet moment I wrap my arms around a cement pole that holds up the slide, and immediately I think of hugging a tree. The mere act of encircling that column of concrete and steel sends me into a rooted state of being. Flash. . . I am in a forest, feeling dark and quiet tree energy.

What is the meaning of life? Joseph Campbell says that is the wrong question. Rather we should ask, what is the experience of being?

FORGIVENESS

that he couldn't help her
bloom into womanhood,
that he did not hold her
heart in his hand nor
cradle her in his arms,

that he did not cherish
her beauty or youth
her intelligence or her hurt places,

that he did not wait or listen
or sew the seeds of partnership:
(growing yearning fighting winning)
in both their blazing hearts, to
create intelligence that between them
was more than they had apart,

that he couldn't see feel cry
enough to stretch out of
his smothered heart's confines,
that he couldn't bless her and keep her
and surrender to her woman's wisdom

HARVEY MILK AND ME

It's a chilly wet night in December. I'm sitting by the fire, wrapping Christmas gifts for my daughter, my son-in-law and grandson Robert. I'm cozy and warm and feeling in the spirit of things. The phone rings and it's my son calling from work.

"Hi Mom, I'm working late. Do you want to go see Harvey Milk? It's the opera tonight. I can't make it".

My silence is loud.

"Do you want to sell the ticket? You can keep the money. Mom are you there?"

I don't want to go out in the cold and I'm pleased with myself for getting the jump on all this wrapping. Oh boy, a hundred dollars would pay for my photographs of the Lake District, or my writing class in December, or a weeks' groceries, although it seems food prices have doubled in the last couple of months. Oh damn, I'll never get a hundred for it anyway, and I'm embarrassed even having a ticket at that price to sell. What with people hungry and homeless and dying of aids,

"O.K.," I say grumpily, "I'll take it. Thanks."

I drag my arthritic feet together, stumble into my raincoat and call for the dog. Bo-Bo is black, wooly, old, a cross between a bear and a wookie. A Bouvier de Flaunders which is just a French sheepdog with a fancy name, and he likes to herd everyone in the house, including my cat L.B., who plaintively puts up with him. I don't want him to pee in the house while I'm gone. It's been raining for a few days and he hates getting wet, so I have to leash him up and drag him outside for a pee. He's such a wimp. He tried to pee in the cat box but got it all over himself and went around emanating of cat piss for a day till I could give him a bath. He's also taken to jumping up onto the dining room table and trying to see through the window whenever he's left alone, knocking every thing off in the process. But it's a miracle how he gets up there in the first place.

So I grab my purse and hustle him into the Taurus, where

43

he plops down on the back seat, scuffling up the old towel I keep there for him so he won't totally destroy the seat cover.

I get down to Van Ness and I'm looking for the Opera House and can't find the damn thing. On the second drive around I see that it's being retro-fitted for earthquake damage, and it's disguised as a construction site. As there is no one around anyway, I put two and two together and come up with the brilliant deduction that the performance must be elsewhere. I pull up to a street light, snatch a look at the ticket and catch the words Orpheum Theatre. Oh God where's the Orpheum. Market and something, I remember.

It's starting to rain again.

Pulling around to McAllister Street I park in a no parking area and jump out looking for someone to ask directions of. Stumbling up the curb and around a concrete pole I catch sight of a slender black woman crossing the street. We speak simultaneously.

"Can you tell me where the Orpheum is?"

"Will you give me and my baby a ride to the battered womans shelter?"

Oh God. I'm stopped short. This is not what I'm here for, is it?

"My husband gets out of jail tomorrow and I gotta get me and my baby out of here. He beat me up before and he'll do it again. The shelter I'm in is full for tomorrow and I have to get away." She gestures nervously, eyes wide and frightened. Her shoulders are drawn together as if to protect her heart.

"Where's the shelter?" I say, knowing she can hear the hesitation in my voice.

" San Mateo," she tells me, taking from her jacket pocket a torn piece of paper, on which is written an address. I see writing but it doesn't register in my brain.

"The cab fare is twenty-one dollars and I don't have it," she says. Her voice has a desperate tone to it.

"Where is San Mateo?" I ask.

"Down near San Jose," says she.

Damn, I don't want to drive to San bloody Mateo. I decide

that if I can sell the ticket I'll give her the money.

"Do you want to come to the Orpheum with me to sell the ticket? Will you show me where it is? I'll give you the money for a cab" I tell her.

"Oh sure."

"You wanna get in first? He's big," referring to BoBo. Will he bite me?"

Well, good point, I think. He has been known to scare the hell out of the mail man.

We get in the car. She guides me, and we park by another no parking sign, jump out, lock the doors and hurry across to the Orpheum Theatre.

"What's your name?" I ask.

"Dee Dee," she says, "What's yours? Wait, watch out for that car!"She grabs my arm, pulls me back from oncoming traffic.

In front of the Orpheum I wave my ticket in the air.

"Great seat." I shout. No one is buying. Two others selling and last minute patrons hurrying in. I pace up and down scanning the streets for potential buyers. Dee Dee in distress, walks away to the cement barrier and looks back, face twisted in anguish.

The gray haired distinguished looking door-man anounces "Curtain going up, no one seated after the performance starts."

A slim dark-blonde haired woman wearing glasses walks up and looks at me.

"How much for your ticket?"

"It's a hundred," I say, "but I'll take fifty great seat"

"I think I can give you forty," she tells me.

I grimace.

"At least I think I've got forty." Doubtfully I look around, and there's no one buying. She starts counting her money.

"Gee, well, I guess I've got thirty seven."

Casting a quick look at Dee Dee, I decide. "OK. It's yours."

"Thanks! Wow, thanks."

I count the money into Dee Dee's hand.

"Bless you." She hugs me and I say, "Be safe."

I walk back to the car and the dog, and when I look around she is gone. The new library is brightly lit. On my left in a storefront window I catch a glimpse of a man's face behind glass. He is handsome and brown and I interpret the look on his face as pain.

I cross over Market, get stuck on Howard, realize I have to go down a couple more blocks, and finally head up toward Mission, Cesar Chavez, and home. Thoughts and feelings rush through me.

Why didn't I take her back to the shelter?Take her home with me, ask if she was hungry, give her more money, give her my phone number? Tears roll down my cheeks as I remember absent fathers and hurt children, remember times of being so desperate I felt crazy. I drive up to the house on the hill thinking about the inequities of life. There but for the grace of god, yeah yeah. Walk in anothers footsteps. Right!

When I awake next morning I had dreamed of helping a friend to compose a Buddhist chant.

HOLDING ON TO IT

The men have been unloading hay into the barn since five a.m. this morning. The first hay truck rolled passed the driveway at midnight. It woke me up with it's particular and persistent sound. Getting out of bed and going over to look out the window I see twin yellow lights flashing down low, along the sides, the larger orange lights up front illuminating the dirt road and the hay barns.

I made a cup of tea and watched for half an hour with my cat L.B., musing about leavings, comings and goings. My girl friend called yesterday to tell me a funny story about a friend of hers who had taken off with the Thanksgiving turkey. She did a Thelma and Louise. Before she knew what she was doing she had grabbed the cooked stuffed plump golden brown, dripping and still warm fowl, thrown a big towel around it, grabbed her car keys,and run out to the driveway. She jumped in the car, threw the turkey in the back, and roared out the driveway giggling hysterically. She split. She left. She was not home. The hell with this shit, she thought. I'm outta here, turkey on the coast, freedom from nonsense. So much of life is non-sense that I'm now actively protecting myself from it.

Now Saturday morning, 9.a.m. they've got the fork lift and are unloading bails of hay. The two men make it look simple; the one with the faded red T-shirt and the gray ponytail on top of the truck, and the other with a beard driving the fork lift. The trucks have been coming here for three or four weeks now and the huge metal barn is nearly filled with hay again. It's the end of summer and forage is being stored for winter feeding for the cows.

When I visited my Mother in England last year before she died of cancer, I was amazed and irritated at how much time she spent chattering away to herself, like the little bird that she was. My step father said to me, "Oh she's like that all the time, I don't even answer back now."

After being with them a week I could understand why she talked to herself. I thought she'd lost it, but she was just holding on to it.

It's comforting to think that we'll have another winter here at Gray View Farm, before looking for another place to live. My daughter and I love the old, gracious farm house that we rented from Dick Gray a year and a half ago: the spacious rooms with high ceilings and large picture windows, that let in wonderful dappled light through the leaves of the pear, peach, and plum trees on the south side, which had been planted when the house was built. Intoxicating to have a kitchen with ample drawers and cupboards, including an airing cupboard.

On the front porch we have put a couple of stuffed easy chairs for viewing the lambs and chicken barns across the way. To the right of the front steps is a raspberry bush, on the left a willow tree. In the back as you come up the steps is a laundry and storage porch with windows looking out onto the fields and foothills of Petaluma.

In the field behind the horses, I see the red roof of the wooden barn looking straight out of a James Wyeth painting. The newer metal barn which the men have been filling with hay again is over to the right, behind the house and in front of the milking sheds.

The owls have been frantic while the barn was being emptied of all the old hay. Now they are back to their usual night patterns, calling to each other in screeches, and swooping between the two barns as they feed their young and give them flying lessons.

The abandoned wooden water tower is where the owls raise their young. It stands in the field across from the house which Dick Gray built for his new bride. The ancient and massive holding barrel is fitted on to the top of the tower. Unused for many a year, the walls are covered with dust and spider webs.

This June I climbed to the top, to photograph the fuzzy, comical hatchlings, who had hatched out on the floor of the barrel, which made a safe haven for the new born owls. To judge by the state of the floor, many generations of nestlings had been born there. Owlets are said to eat their own weight in rodents in a single night, and along with the white spatters of excrement were neat pellets of regurgitated fur, feather and bone from many field mice, and about a hundred tiny bird and animal skulls. I gathered these tiny skulls and kept them in a small wooden box. At one time there were six owls of varying sizes all perched up on the rim of the old barrel at the top of the water tower. My heart was in my mouth looking at those heart shaped beautiful self contained faces, and, as they couldn't fly yet, they were captive to my camera.

Now September, the fields are pale golden brown. The two ponds have dried up, leaving only a muddy bottom for the frogs. A neighbor came to the door last Saturday looking for his falcon, and to tell me that a cow was stuck in the mud. On noting my garden he allowed that he hadn't put one in this year.

The dairy barns with old milking machinery growing rusty are on the back five acres. A few cows are still here but 'Gray View Estates' as the new housing development is named, is steadily creeping up Corona Avenue, house frames popping up like mushrooms, all the way to the Pavaroti's Nursery. There is to be a new school on the grounds. We are looking for the next plot of land to nurture. I called Jose the ranch manager to tell him about the cow. He has seen his family grow up here, and said his wife Petra hated to leave the old farmhouse, the house that has soaked up the loving and grieving of a couple of lifetimes.

Last week a man came pedaling by on a bicycle up the dirt road. I was out in the garden and he asked me if they still did milking here. Said he was out here milking fifteen years ago for Dick Gray, the owner. Said he was visiting his sister, and back home in Iowa he was growing soy beans.

Went to the city last week with my sister visiting and recovering from a stroke. She looks well though she tells me she sometimes puts her knickers on her head instead of the other end. Gabbing over a latte in Starbucks, next door we see tucked into a large doorway, a green sleeping bag with boots placed close by, a gray haired head poking out the top, partially covered with clothes, piled on against the cold.

Last week my son flew me over the land. The house and barns were gone. There are hundreds of people living in new suburbs. 'Gray View Farm' is no more. Wendell Berry echoes my heart when he says, "Telling stories and making soil are two good things to do."

HUSBANDRY

In Valley Ford
Michelle makes a garden

> *sings a blessing*
> *plants a prayer*
> *tills the soil   adds compost*
> *water   thanks god for water .*
> *renews the land*
> *french intensive*
> *resurrects hallowed ground*

sows the earth   down on her knees
seeds through fingers sifting.

    corn   melons   peas
    basil   arugula   pole beans
    sunflowers,   six
    different kinds
    spaghetti squash   gourmet lettuce
    tomatoes in copious profusion

she knows how to speak with gardens.
husbandry is in her bones
for her, a garden is sufficient
she gives it full measure
and brilliant is her harvest

    swallows whirl and swoop
    butterflies honey bees   hummingbirds
    pollinating
    silvery waves of grass blowing on the hill
    are meditation

    from ancestral burial grounds
    there come whispers
    urgent echoings
    care for the land
    honor the land.

Spider Woman
and The Glass Fairy
Rosemary Sheppard

ROSEMARY SHEPPARD

"Although my childhood was spent in such diverse places as Indonesia, Louisiana, and Colorado, I was born on a California farm, shortly before World War II, a time of war news, blackout curtains, recycling tins, absent fathers, rationing, and the invention of margarine. Margarine didn't come as it does now in yellow cubes or plastic cartons, but rather as a white substance, encased in thick cellophane with yellow food coloring to be kneaded into it. Margarine stayed in our lives, even after butter became available again. It was much cheaper, and health gurus said it was better for us. Later, shopping for my own family, I went straight for the fake stuff. I even spread it on the bread I became famous for baking. But when my beloved Wolfgang and I retired to Surprise Valley, a remote paradise in the northeast corner of California, whose countryside is dotted with sheep and cattle, we liberated ourselves from jobs, cities and margarine.

Conventional wisdom says, a writer should write about what she knows. It seemed wise to me when I was eighteen and knew nothing, so I decided to put off writing until I had some age on me and some wisdom. What I didn't know was that I would know even less when I was fifty, that wisdom didn't arrive automatically with age. Waiting so long was, by far, the worst mistake I ever made. Unlike other mistakes, there were no obvious consequences such as broken relationships, poverty, jail, or poor feng shui. There was only nothing. I began to write at fifty, reading my writings to any poor soul who happened to be around. All my listeners were encouraging and compassionate, until a glimmer of wisdom cut through the euphoria of creation, and I began to seek out other writers, writers who could tell me when a story didn't work and suggest how to fix it. If any young writers wish to partake of my wisdom, I will tell them to write it—now."

Ms. Sheppard has been published in The Butterfly Chronicles, and the Cosmic Unicorn.

SPIDER WOMAN

One Morning when time was just beginning, Spider Woman ran along the pathway where the sky meets the earth just as the sun began to rise. She ran West and she ran South. She ran North and East. When she had done what she had to do at the Four Corners and Sun was all the way up she began to spin a web.

She worked all of that day and through the night, and when Sun rose again the next morning, no one on earth could see him because the sky was completely covered with cobweb.

When Sun realized that no one on earth could see his light or feel his warmth, he was very angry and tried to burn up the web. But every time a strand of her web began to burn Spider woman would scurry out and spit on the burning strand. And so her web became even stronger.

After awhile Sun sank beneath the earth and Moon rose to shine her silver light on earth. But Spider Woman's web kept moonlight and cold away from the earth as it had kept away sunlight and warmth. Moon became very angry and called upon Wind to come and blow the cobweb away. But every time Wind lifted an edge of the cobweb, Spider Woman scurried out and glued it down. And her web became even stronger.

On the earth the birds and animals and people were very unhappy, because the web kept warmth and cold and light and darkness away from the earth.

"The sky is our domain," the birds said to each other. "We must remove the web or we will not be able to fly."

"I am the strongest," said Eagle, "I will remove the cobweb."

"Sun could not burn the cobweb and wind could not blow it," said Sparrow. "You are strong, but Sun and Wind are stronger than you."

"Sun and Wind are strong," said Starling, "But we are many. If all of the birds on earth attack the web, it will fall."

Even Sparrow agreed that this was a good plan. So all the birds on earth rose together and flew into the web. The web billowed out like a sail in the wind when they hit it, but the web did not break. And the birds, like a million flies, were stuck in Spider Woman's web.

Now all the animals on earth gathered to see what could be done about the cobweb.

"Grass will not grow if there is no warmth and light," said Antelope. "We must do something."

"I am strongest," said Bear. "I will take down the web."

"You are strong," said Rabbit, "but Sun and Wind could not take down the web and they are stronger than you. And all of the birds on earth flew into the web and now they are stuck."

"Yes," said Buffalo, "But we are larger and stronger than the birds. If we all hit the web at once, it will fall."

So all of the animals on earth ran together at the web and when they hit the web it billowed out like a sail in the wind. But it did not break, and all of the animals on earth were stuck on Spider Woman's web.

Then First Woman came and stood in front of the web. She stood there for such a long time that Spider Woman came out on her web, and spoke to her. "Are you going to gather all of the people on earth to see if you can break my web?" she asked.

"Oh no," said First Woman. "Your web is lovely. If I could weave like that, my children could have beautiful warm clothes to wear. How did you manage to attach it to the Four Corners of the sky?"

"Only I can weave the sky," answered Spider Woman. "If you are going to weave we will have to build a loom." And First Woman and Spider Woman walked away together, leaving the cobweb to hang between the earth and the sun.

After awhile Sun dried up the strands of the web and Wind picked it up gently and scattered the birds and animals back across the world. But Spider Woman didn't mind. She could always spin a new web.

THE GLASS FAIRY

The wind howled and whirled glass chips of snow into Buddy's face, as he struggled the few yards from the parking lot to the entrance of his apartment building. His numb fingers faltered and fumbled with his keys that hung from a retractable chain on his belt. When he found the key to the iron gate that guarded his apartment building, it seemed a century passed before he was able to insert it into the lock and stumble into the dingy lobby.

Another key unlocked his mail box. Bills and junk mail as usual. But on the long table the mail carrier used, to place packages too large for the locked boxes, a package addressed to him stood. His lips formed a smile on his frozen face. Some great luck at last.

The Science Fiction and Fantasy Book Club had sent the newest De Lint. He cradled the heap of mail and the cardboard package against his chest, and prepared for the last trek of this journey, the three flights up to his apartment. Just then something pricked his skin from an inner pocket. The glass figurine!

Earlier he had discovered it by a drift of new snow, like the discarded toy of a careless child. He had been incredibly lucky not to have smashed it under the massive wheels of his truck, while backing into his place on the company lot, or crushed it with his boots when he jumped out of the cab. He had drawn off his bulky gloves and carefully plucked the fragile object out of its icy bed. Gently, he buttoned it into the pocket of his flannel shirt where its chill pierced his clothing like an aching heart.

Before he started up the stairs and down the dimly lit corridor of the third floor, he shifted his mail to carry it under his arm, and extracted the key to his apartment. But when he pushed open the door at last, and reached to turn on the lights, he clapped his hand over his nose and mouth and backed out. His apartment stank—of mildew, stale beer and the ghost of ancient take-outs, but most of all it stank of garbage, overflowing from a can in the middle of the living room.

With a convulsive shudder he slammed the door hard, so the brass number thirty-one, which hung suspended from a single nail, rattled dangerously before it fell to the faded black and white tile floor. The stench, of neglected garbage denied its freedom, struggled against the closed door and began to seep between the cracks into the hallway. . . reaching for him.

Buddy removed his grease stained Cub's baseball cap, and rubbed at that place on his head where the dark curly hair was beginning to thin. He wasn't ready for the garbage he had forgotten to take out a week ago. After crawling his eighteen-wheeler through a hundred miles of blizzard, he was tired. He needed a bath. He needed his bed, not his garbage. He could leave and find a motel for the night and deal with this problem in the morning. But that would mean going back out into the storm.

He drew in a deep breath, held it, pushed open the door and rushed through the living room, straight for the aluminum-framed sliding window. It resisted. Snow and ice packed along its outside edges sealed it effectively against normal human effort. But adrenaline was pumping through his blood. He gave a heroic tug and the window slid reluctantly open, letting in a blast of cold fresh air. He released his breath and gulped in a lung full of the winter night. Holding his breath again, he hastily wrestled the garbage can out the door and down the hall to the trash disposal slot.

At least the neighbors hadn't called in the Health Department, like they had on that poor old woman who kept pigeons in her apartment. He slumped down on a sagging orange and black plaid sofa and tugged at his snow soaked boots. In spite of the freezing wind tearing through his apartment and out the front door, a smell of garbage lingered. Maybe his place had always smelled that way and he had just never noticed.

Buddy wrinkled his nose, but he got up and closed the door. If his neighbors hadn't noticed the filth before, there was no point in bringing it to their attention now. He looked around in disgust. How had things gotten to be so bad? The trucking office had more personality, with its wall-wide bulletin board and fly specked pinup calendars, than his apartment. His walls were bare except for a red thumbtack where once a calendar had hung next to his phone. His bedroom wasn't much better. He threw his boots in the direction of the closet door. For the first time since his brother married and moved out ten years ago, he really looked at the room he slept in. Except for two drooping bookcases filled with a colorful collection of paperback science fiction, a chipped green dresser and a bed without a spread or headboard, it was sparsely furnished. Next to the bed stood a plain brown bedside table, with a crookneck lamp, three paperback novels, a TV guide, and two pairs of reading glasses piled on its inadequate surface. A digital alarm clock sat on the floor just out of reach of a sleepy arm.

What his place needed was some pictures on the walls to brighten it up. He still had the Cub's poster his nephew gave him last Christmas rolled up on the closet shelf and he could pick up a company calendar next week at work.

Happy with his decision to decorate, Buddy tossed his cap on the dresser and tore off the cardboard wrapping of his new book. First, a long hot shower, a cup of instant coffee, and then, he'd treat himself to an all night read.

Buddy read the first page of the book and then read it again before he remembered the blue glass figurine tucked in the pocket of his flannel work shirt. Like the idiot he was learning to believe he was, he had rumpled up the shirt and thrown it on the bathroom floor. Damn! If it were broken. . .

In seconds he was holding the figurine under the bedside lamp, turning it to look for cracks or chips. He had never seen anything so tiny, so fragile. It looked like a sleeping child. . . no, a sleeping fairy with wings folded along the curved back, and teeny antenna curled above the smooth forehead. He had seen glass blown into wonderful shapes in the gift stores attached to truck stops, but this... this was art! And he had been lucky again. Rough treatment hadn't injured the pretty little thing.

He couldn't leave the glass fairy on the bedside table. Its varnished surface was too crowded. Buddy padded across the room to the dresser and pulled out two blue-bordered handkerchiefs. He folded the handkerchiefs until they made a thick pad, and set it on the dresser. He lay the figurine gently on the improvised bed and covered it with the other handkerchief. It was a nutty thing to do, but if he couldn't be crazy in his own room, in his own apartment, when no one could see, it was too bad.

"Goodnight Miss Fairy," he whispered.

He woke in the morning with thoughts of flowers, of spring bouquets with white daisies, pinks and those dark blue. . . geraniums or something. He yawned, rolled out of bed and padded over to the window. Snow covered the apartment parking lot transforming the cars into a row of identical sparkling white hills. But at least the storm was over, and he could drive to the mall first thing and buy some flowers.

Spring flowers in January are expensive, but Buddy bought out the florist, a short bald man who walked on his toes. He grinned at Buddy.

"I guess you'll be too busy today to watch the playoffs," he said, carefully wrapping the bouquets in waxy paper, inserting instructions and a little packet of preservative into each one.

The playoffs! How could he have forgotten the playoffs? The guys were at the bar right now yelling at each other while the pre-game shows blared statistics and gossip about the players. And here he was buying flowers for his apartment! It was a good thing the gang couldn't see him. Buddy hurriedly paid the man, and with his arms full of flowers, rushed across to the deli for beer and pizza.

Molly, the woman who ran the delicatessen, raised her thick dark eyebrows when she saw the flowers.

But she only asked, "Sausage pizza and a six-pack of Miller's for watching the football game?"

"No, I'm kind of tired of pizza, Molly. Maybe, I'll try something different."

Buddy looked into the long glass display case and was surprised to see at least two dozen items he had never noticed before. He pointed to something that looked like a pie. "What's that?"

"Quiche, broccoli quiche. I make it myself. It's quite good." She pulled the quiche from the case and began to wrap it up. She looked up, saw Buddy's face, and laughed. "It's good! I promise you. If you don't like it, I'll fix you a sausage pizza for free."

Buddy watched her plump white fingers deftly wrap the quiche with string and butcher paper. When she handed him the neat package, he handed her a bouquet of pink carnations.

"Thanks Buddy," she said, laughing. She put them in a glass except for one that she stuck behind her ear so it nestled in the thick mass of her black hair. "I guess your new girlfriend won't miss a few carnations."

Buddy blushed. So that was why the florist was leering at him. And now, he certainly couldn't explain to Molly that he was buying the flowers for a glass figurine. "Bye Molly," he mumbled, and hurried out of the mall.

Flowers bloomed in coffee cans, peanut butter jars, beer bottles, on top of the refrigerator, and on the medicine cabinet in the bathroom. Buddy took special pains with one small vase, the only one he owned. He trimmed the stems making what his mother used to call, 'an arrangement'. He carried this bouquet into his bedroom and placed it carefully on the chest of drawers between his cap and the glass fairy's bed.

"Here," he said to the figurine, "are your flowers." With his finger he gently pushed back the handkerchief so he could see his tiny treasure. It looked different. Not quite so blue, not so cold. He shook his head. Of course, it wasn't cold. It wasn't lying in a snow bank in a winter storm. He wondered how it had gotten there. But strange as that was, the really strange thing was, he wanted to talk to it. He shook his head again and walked back into the living room and switched on the TV to watch the football game. Tomorrow while he was driving to Cleveland would be plenty of time to think about glass fairies.

Two days later when Buddy returned from Cleveland he went straight to the bedroom without taking off his jacket, to check on the blue glass fairy he had left curled up on the chest of drawers. He looked down at the handkerchief bed, and abruptly turned around and walked back into the living room and sank down heavily on the sofa. He held his head in his hands for a few minutes before he slowly got up and went in to look again.

The tiny figurine lay under the handkerchief where he had left her, but now she was straight instead of curled, and white except for her hair, dress, and wings, all of which were an iridescent sparkling blue.

He was crazy. It came of living alone! He should go down to the bar, play a little pool and forget about the glass fairy. He shrugged off his jacket and sat down on the bed to take off his boots.

The kind of person he needed wasn't down at the bar playing pool. A picture of plump white fingers came to his mind. Molly? The woman at the deli? What made him think of Molly? He wasn't going to run down to the mall and bother Molly with his problems. No way was he going to do that.

Buddy looked bleakly around. If he was crazy he should go to the doctor. No, what he should do is paint the living room. Yes, and buy some new furniture, a sofa and one of those lounge chairs and an entertainment center so his TV didn't have to sit on a cart in the middle of the room.

"Good night, Miss Fairy," he said to the figurine, Later, when he went to bed. "I'll get busy with fixing up our apartment in the morning."

Buddy was at the furniture store when it opened. He wasn't anticipating any trouble making a decision. He was a simple man with simple tastes. A dark brown sofa and a lounge chair to match, and of course, the entertainment center. Black would be nice.

"May I help you?" An elegantly attired salesman had approached noiselessly on the thick carpet.

"I would like to see some sofas."

"Of course. Follow me if you please."

As Buddy followed the salesman he began to realize that he was in the wrong store. The rich woods, the sparkling crystal belonged in the big houses on Snob Hill, not in his little apartment on the outskirts of Industrial Park. He would have to go to a different mall.

Then he saw the love seat. It stood on delicate legs of dark wood, had a high rounded back, and a seat so narrow any lovers foolish enough to sit on it would have to sit straight or slide off. It was upholstered with red roses on a plush green background.

"I'll take that." he heard himself say to the salesman. "But, I think I'll need to have a coffee table to go with it. And some vases. I want to see some crystal vases." He closed his mouth with a snap, but it was too late.

"Yes Sir!" the salesman purred. "Right this way, Sir."

Several weeks later Buddy was shopping again, this time for harp music to play on his new stereo system. As he walked by the deli, he saw Molly taking a break at one of the little round tables where people sat to drink the exotic coffee she served.

He went in and sat across from her, his eyes a mirror to her welcoming smile. "Well, that's cheerful," she said, pointing with her chin at the Hawaiian print shirt he was wearing.

"Yeah. Well, what are you reading?"

"Jack of Kinrowan by Charles De Lint."

"You like De Lint?"

"I've got everything he's ever written. I like the way he has of getting real people mixed up with fairy folk. Sometimes after I've read one of his books I start wondering about stuff."

She laughed, "You know that pair of crows that hang around outside the mall? Sometimes I wonder if they aren't the Crow Girls— you know the shapeshifters."

"Ahh, Molly. . . you know that time last January after we had that big storm, and I came in here with all those flowers and you thought I had a girlfriend. Well I didn't. . . have a girlfriend. . . I mean. . ."

He began to pour out the story of finding the glass fairy. He told Molly about going to work and returning to find Miss Fairy changed, how sometimes it was the color of her hair and clothes, sometimes her position, sitting or standing or lying in the little handkerchief bed he made for her. One time she had been a 'he'-dressed in green, and smoking a little glass pipe. And the worst thing was, he knew he was crazy because he couldn't help buying things. Crazy things like a blue velvet smoking jacket when he didn't even smoke, and shirts with flowers all over them, and furniture.

When he was finished Molly looked at him, her eyes thoughtful. "But is that so bad? I mean is it so awful to try different stuff? Even food...Is it so awful to eat something besides pizza?"

She glanced over to the counter where several customers were beginning to mill around discontentedly. "Don't go away. I'll wait on these people, then close up and we can talk some more." She got up and left him alone with her book.

Buddy watched her walk away. It wasn't so much pizza or quiche that brought him into the deli. It was a pair of dark gold-flecked eyes and hips that rolled enticingly under a tight polyester uniform. He sighed, pulled the book toward him and plunged again into the story of fairies and magic in Ottawa.

When he looked up again, the gate had been drawn across

the deli's doorway, the counters had been cleaned, and the floor swept. Molly put two styrofoam cups of steaming coffee and two huge pieces of black speckled yellow cake on the little table.

"I'm going to have to throw this poppy seed cake out tomorrow," she said, as she plopped herself down in the chair opposite Buddy, and took a plastic fork full of cake. "You know, I think I know where it came from. . . your fairy. It came from Canada. Blew across in that big storm we had in January." She tapped the book lying on the table.

"Come on, that's just a story."

"No, I'm serious. Think about it. That's not fiction and you're not crazy. You're living with a real live fairy." She took another forkful of cake and watched as he played nervously with his fork.

"You might be right," he said thoughtfully. Its a nutty idea, but no crazier than what's going on at my place!"

"You're going to have to get rid of it. Or you *will* go crazy." Then she reached across the table and put her hand on his arm. "Take me to your apartment. Show it to me."

She looked like a little girl begging for a pony ride.

"Okay," Buddy pushed back his chair and stood up. "Let's go."

Looking into Buddy's apartment was like looking through a kaleidoscope into a universe of swirling color. The walls were papered with tiny blue flowers entwined with unlikely leaves, and hung with paintings and prints of roses, lilacs, marigolds, poppies, and lilies-of-the-valley, framed in glittering silver. The floor was covered with a deep piled baby blue Chinese rug, bordered with pink and yellow flowers. Furniture and cushions upholstered in crimson and emerald satin crowded the room. Crystal vases held pink and yellow roses on every available surface. Sweet piping of flute music wafted from the stereo system. Molly backed away.

"It *is* magic," she whispered. "It's like a real fairy land. It's scary."

"It's my apartment. It's where I live, and you're my guest.

So come on in." He gave her hand a little tug and pulled her into the living room kicking the door closed behind her. And immediately he felt remorse. What if Molly was really frightened? He put a square hand on each of her shoulders and looked in her eye

"Are you really scared? Do you want to leave? You're the first person I've had in the place since January. But if you want to leave that's okay."

"No, of course. . ." Then her head jerked, her body arched and she began to scream.

"What's the matter? Oh my God, what's the matter?" He pulled her toward him and suddenly her body relaxed and fell heavily into his arms.

"I'm all right now. Something or someone pulled my hair. I guess she doesn't want me here."

"Well I want you here! It's my place after all!" The stereo began to screech like a chorus of banshees.

"Jesus!" Buddy took a step to turn it off and fell to the floor.

"Don't get up!" Molly shouted. She ran to turn off the CD player. Then in the sudden silence she knelt next to Buddy.

"Your shoelaces are tied together. Shh. . . don't say anything," she whispered in his ear. "Fix your shoes, but while you're doing that think about the rules."

"What rules?"

"The rules that govern the intercourse between fairies and humans, of course. You have to play by the rules or your shoelaces will be tangled for the rest of your life."

Ohoooo...whooooo...whooooo...a wolf howled and then creak...creak, a rusty door opened in a haunted house and somewhere a one-hinged shutter banged in the wind.

Molly's eyes grew big. Buddy grabbed her hand. "Miss Fairy found my Halloween tape that all. It's ok."

He lay back on the floor and closed his eyes. Ha ha...ha ha...hee hee hee...and the tape player continued its melody of spooky noises.

Finally he opened his eyes, looked at Molly and winked. He

stood up, first checking his shoe laces and walked over to the window. He turned and addressed the room.

"There's a full moon tonight, Miss Fairy. And you owe me something. I saved your life and you owe me three wishes." He cocked his head as if he were listening to a voice inside his skull then he nodded. "OK. One life, one wish. It'll do."

He opened the window wide. The parking lot outside was bare of snow for the first time in weeks and bathed in moon glow. There was something in the air that smelled of spring to come.He turned back to the room and declared in a loud voice. "I wish that you'd return to where you came from and..." he hesitated, "God speed."

With a loud clap every vase in the house overturned spilling water and plants on several thousand dollars worth of rugs. The window slammed shut. Whooo...whoo... the CD player continued to howl.

Then suddenly the apartment was silent and empty.
Buddy grinned at Molly.

"Let's get this mess cleaned up and then go out for pizza." He shook his head. "Now that was a dumb idea. Who needs pizza when they can have quiche or, I know, there's that new Thai place that opened up on Orchard Street. Let's head over there for dinner."

He took her hand and gently pulled her towards him. "You know," he said, wondering at the sophistication of the remark he was about to utter, "I think I've exchanged one enchantress for another."

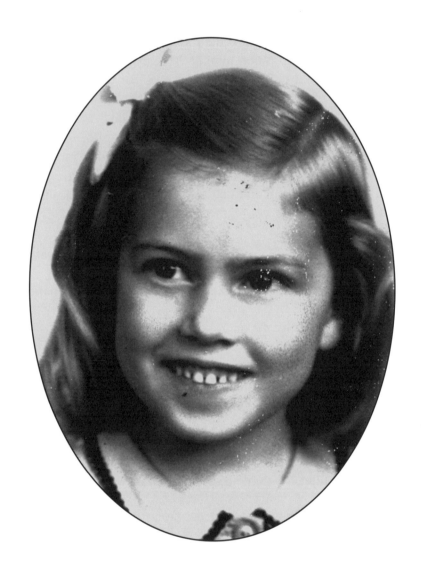

A Trio of Politically
Incorrect Tales

Karla Andersdatter

KARLA ANDERSDATTER

Karla Andersdatter is a West Coast author, born in San Francisco, California, the year Hitler was forcing Jews, Gypsies, and Poles into concentration camps in Europe. She remembers the blackouts along the coast of California and the naval ship yards in Puget Sound during World War II, the sound of Franklin Delano Roosevelt's voice each night, as she and her family listened to the war reports over the radio. She learned to read and write in a two room schoolhouse in 1943, her mother the teacher in the next room.

Ms. Andersdatter describes her work as follows: *"My life is my work, and every life is derived from the times of our birth, and the people in our surroundings, as well as our genes. For me, life is an organic process within which I struggle and learn, both from what I perceive and feel, as well as what I do and what I am. I have been fortunate to experience a multitude of remarkable people, amazed to raise a son and daughter, delighted to have participated in the lives of four grandchildren, and lived to see 14 books published. I am fascinated by words, and literary artists, intrigued by the world of the intellect and haunted by the almighty forces of nature. Wherever I walk, I am shocked, befuddled, absorbed, intrigued, delighted. This is what feeds my imagination."*

Ms. Andersdatter has written two novels, a collection of fairytales, seven volumes of poetry, three children's books, and a novella, published in 1999. She has been published in the San Francisco Chronicle, The Pacific Sun, and the New York Times as well as many literary magazines. She has worked as a publisher, editor, teacher, artist, and storyteller. *"It is the artist in me, in whatever form she takes, who wants me to live, who brings joy to others and cleanses my emotions, who gives meaning to my life and allows me to listen to my heart, to believe the best, and find compassion for the worst in myself and in others. I believe that this creative force needs to be nurtured and used to its fullest extent during my lifetime, lest it become crippled and tortured, or turn in on itself to grow cruel, conniving, or destructive. It is always the Muse who rids one of darkness."*

SIR ERRANT THE WICKET
a short politically incorrect and decidedly wicked tale

In a square castle above the sea lived a great English lord called Errant the Wicket. He claimed to be of English blood and took on the superficial trappings of civilization. He wore royal garments to sit at the table of the King. He spoke in high and elegant language, and could quaff great pitchers of ale and devour shoulders of beef and whole ducks with the best of the knights.

He was renowned for feats of strength in jousting, bicycle riding, and games of futbol and teness, which the King had recently invented (being bored with lawn teness and cricket) for the delight and entertainment of his noble throng. In all manner of things, Errant the Wicket did indeed fulfill the requisite qualifications of an English Lord.

Yet deep in his veins ran the savage blood of the Hun and the Viking, ah yes, deep in his heart he was a barbarian. Whereas other lords wrote poetry for their ladye loves, went on crusades and dragon slaying missions for their Gwynneveres and Genevieves, this cruel lord did lure them into his square castle by the sea, enchant them with his magic potions (which were kept in long dark green bottles, hidden in the corner behind the kitchen cutlery) and then ravish them with their mildly inebriated consent.

This manner of sport continued until one cold afternoon he

saw a ladye, fleet of foot and light of heart, by the name of Carlotta. Carlotta was not an English ladye although she often entertained the court with her strange manner of expression and ready good humor. Carlotta was a savage and rumored to be related to gypsies!

It may have been the deep call of her barbarian blood that found an answering stir within Sir Errant, for when he saw her, he became excited with the anticipation of luring her to his square castle by the sea. Upon reaching the inner quarters of his abode, and uncorking the green bottles to pour his wicked love potion into her glass, he became so entranced looking into her wild eyes, that he poured the magic liquid into both glasses instead of hers alone. And Carlotta, when Sir Errant turned his back for a moment added her own ancient herbs of love, so that when they drank, they both became enamoured, and lured each other into Errant the Wicket's lordly boudoir. So it was they stayed that way (enamoured) for many years.

This strange accident of fate did not change Sir Errant's behavior however. He continued to joust, play futbol, and teness, to speak in elegant language, and dress in a lordly manner. All this would have been all right except he did not adopt the lordly manner of a Knight in Love.

He was known to go for days without riding to his ladye love's wagon. He was seen quaffing ale in public places, instead of courting his ladye with love songs and quatrains of verse.

If Carlotta had been a noble ladye, she would have told him, "Prithee, be gone! For thou hast shown thyself by action and demeanor unworthy of my favors. I shall take me to a nunnery."

However Carlotta was a pagan and she spoke in simple phrases. She spoke to Sir Errant thusly, "You are a real son-of-a-bitch, and if you don't change and treat me right, you can go get laid somewhere else."

Whereupon, Sir Errant the Wicket did put forth an unlordly, miserably intended effort to seemingly mend his wicked ways, until his bad blood took over again. Finally after many repetitions and variations of the preceding conversation and the concomitant attempted upgrading of Errant's lordliness, Carlotta became most exasperated. In fact you might say she waxed wroth.

"Errant," she shouted, "I'm leaving. Tomorrow I'm going back to the gypsy wagon, and camp out. You can sit around and pick your nose for all I care."

"How camest thou to this decision, my ladye love?" quoth Sir Errant?"

"I'm tired of futbol, teness, and the whole damn court!" yelled Carlotta.

"Thou waxeth wroth over the strangest irrelevancies."

"Thou speaketh another language." Carlotta sighed. "Write me a letter while I am gone, for I shall surely miss you." And to her credit Carlotta did shed a tear and kissed him good-bye fondly.

So it came to pass, that she went away in her red gypsy wagon, to which Sir Errant had hitched the horses. She stayed away for many days and many nights. And all that time, Sir Errant did not set his pen to paper, for he was too engrossed in kingly sport of great import, (such as futbol and teness), to give a bit of joy to the ladye who had loved him so long and loud.

And so it was that Carlotta waxed wroth again, and used all her anger to make a hex on Sir Errant. In her far away gypsy camp she mixed a brew, stirred the pot, and cast the spell.

"Never again shall Sir Errant the Wicket hear words fall from my lips. Until such time as he enscribes to me a letter proclaiming his love and affection, he shall receive word of me only through another's lips, for his is a dastardly and selfish spirit, and he is a blackguard." (Carlotta used elegant language only when casting spells, which is the way of gypsies and witches.) And from that day forward Sir Errant the Wicket lived the life of a Knight in a noble court, never quite understanding how it was he felt cross and crabby more often than not, and why he only received second hand words and no love from his layde.

The end of the story, or as the Shoshoni say,
'the rat's tale fell off'.

A RARE OBJEFACT

Mindalia stretched in the compuchair. Her neck was tired and her long earthen hair fell to one side as she stretched and breathed deeply. The evaluators were kind people to be sure. They spoke softly and smiled a lot. But she wasn't sure she wanted to be here any more.

She was over half a century old, and most Ermegites chose to leave their stations after the age of 50. But Mindalia had a particular talent which had somehow slipped through all the genetic engineering over the centuries. Granted, they had tried to eliminate this trait since the year 2000, but it had not yet been entirely eradicated from the Ermegites, even after concentrated efforts and extensive genetic research. By the year 2500 it had, however, become so unusual and distinct a characteristic, that the Scientobjefacts became increasingly intrigued with it.

They began intense studies to identify the specific effects of this emotionally distressing character of the Ermegites. By the year 2948, the year Mindalia was born, she was put under long term life study, and her history was followed carefully. She was identified as one of the Antiquated Objefacts, and it was predicted she would be a misfit and the cause of social upheaval wherever she worked. Her talent was memory. She remembered her own personal history, from present and past lives, and she remembered it as an emotional hologram. She could describe it in intimate detail with words, so acutely descriptive, that she shocked her listeners.

The planet Earth had indeed evolved into a remarkable and efficient organization of Planned Communities.

ERMEG PLANCO (The Earthen-Memory Genetically Planned Community) was one of three genetically planned communities. The other two were PLANCOG PLANCO (Planetary-Consciousness-Genetically Planned Community) and SUPICOG PLANCO (Superficial-Image-Minding Commercially-Genetic Planned Community).

Mindalia rubbed her neck and returned to the task at hand. She was being trained by a Supicog Citizen and was reading the instructions on the Employment Placement Study Group file. *"All of us hear so much spoken about our personality. We have some idea of what is meant by the word, yet few of us would venture to try to give a simple description of it."* Mindalia smiled to herself.

"What is this 'we' shit?" she thought. She began reading again, desperately trying to focus on the content of the Employment Placement Training File, which continued *"Everyone wants to be highly thought of by friends and by all with whom he comes in contact."* Is this true? Mindalia questioned. Can it be true that everyone wants to be highly thought of? What if I don't want to be thought of at all? What if I only want to be embraced?

She continued reading: *"You might roughly divide personality into two parts: the outward one which we call our appearance, and the inner one which we may call character. Strangers judge you entirely by your apearance. When you come into an office for the first time, you are quickly sized up by the person who is interviewing you. He glances at you and almost unconsciously forms an opinion. . ."*

Mindalia glanced at the time measuring device mounted on the computer, and then looked around the room. There were no windows in the employment room, which was carpeted and quiet except for the sound of softly clicking keys. There were several other trainees taking the job skills class, and she noticed how dutifully they were reading the training manual. She blushed, realizing she was the only one who had paused in the activity of completing the task. Surely that would be noted by the time-measurement device on the computer. *Unfocused attention is one of the failings of the Ermegites.* She remembered reading that in Genetics 2920 A, at the Earthen University.

It was that disturbingly accurate photographic memory of hers. A memory like that was usually part of the Scientobjefact genetic structure. She sighed, realizing she was not only an Ermegite, full of emotion and holgraphic memory, but an also part Objefact, (and an antiquated one at that), one that was exquisitely intelligent with that kind of disturbing intellect that made most earthlings turn away from her, unless they were of the scientobject genetic structure. Almost finished though, almost finished. Now that she was half a century old, she could make her choice about life or dream state whenever she wanted.

Returning to the task at hand, Mindalia read, *"Of course it is your hope that this first impression is a good one. Whether it is favorable or not depends upon whether you have the same idea of what an attractive appearance is as your interviewer. The first thing he looks for is a neat, tidy, harmoniously -groomed person. This generally means simple grooming with coat, dress or suit, hat, shoes, gloves, all to match. Your hair, of course, should be neatly set."*

If she had not had to ride 55 miles this morning along the electric motorway, locked into the lane she had entered that morning, until she exited an hour later, her mood would have definitely been improved, as well as her aching shoulders and back. Honestly, she could not understand the way she did not fit into the world the way it was. Nothing seemed to match her own inner artistry, which was not 'matching', and certainly not harmonious at all times! Oh, well, the evaluators were definitely trying to help, and she definitely believed they wanted to help. Definitely! She noticed in her inner mind how 'definitely' was one of her overused words.

"The way you talk makes a strong impression upon a person whose profession it is to interview people. Are your words

73

firm? Do they show a quiet, easy self-confidence? Do you hold your head up, have a smile on your face when you speak? Is there a minimum of make-up, yet sufficient to show the good lines of your face?" Is this for real? she thought, glancing in the mirrors that covered the walls behind the computer table. There was no smile on her face. *"If the firm you are calling upon is a good one, if it is a place where you are anxious to work, then remember that the personnel director is very careful to select only those people who will fit into this organization. When he talks to you, don't interrupt him. Let him finish each statement or question and then answer simply, clearly, and pleasantly."*

Why did she hate reading this she wondered, longing for a breath of air, longing for a window, a view, anything but this color-ful screen and its innocuous words, unending words, words, words, words, she typed. . .then hit the delete button, as she noticed a monitor coming her way.

"May I help you in any way?" cooed the small SUPICOG monitor, with her waxen smile and rosy cheeks.

"No," Mindalia answered, forcing a smile. Then, lowering her head quickly, she resumed her typing. *"Do you feel you are making a good impression?"* Mindalia giggled softly, and then continued. *All this an experienced personnel director takes in at once. Keep this in mind. If you have made a good impression, the interviewer wants you to work in his organization. Almost unconsciously he wants to help you secure the position that you seek. You have won the greater part of the interview with a good impression. Your good personality has carried over to your interviewer so that he becomes your friend."*

Mindalia suddenly realized that all the vocabulary in the universe didn't matter if you were utterly unemployable in this new world of space travel and star war controls. She typed the date, September 15, 2999. Almost the new millenia. How had she arrived at this place, on this date, and did she want to remain?

She had a choice. If she didn't want to fit into an appropri-ate mental pattern, she could go into the 'restful' mode, the retire-ment mode, and eventually depart her body, leaving it to be harvested in the usual manner: usable parts being distributed as needed, and the rest shredded for the reprocessing plant.The PLANCOGS had the reprocessing plants organized impeccably, efficiently, and they stood ready at all times.

She watched the smiling SUPICOG monitor, and sighed. "I'll stay awhile longer," she thought, "write a few stories before I leave the planet."

She wouldn't starve. She could type.

Please note that bold type indicates excerpts from the California State Worker's Comp Training Literature.

FOREST MOTHER

My grandmother told me this story when I was a child, and who it was that told it to her I cannot say. I only know it is a true story, but then you may not believe in the truth.

When my grandmother was young there were many forests in the land. The trees were old and full of magic. They had never known the touch of ax or chain saw. There was no need to cut down the forest then. The people of the village lived by the sea. Their houses were made of earth and stone. They gathered dung for fuel, and ate nuts, berries and root plants that were easily cultivated in the rich soil. No one came to the forest, and no one bothered the village.

The village children were named the names of birds, after the winged creatures who nested in the trees and by the shore. The villagers believed the birds to be magic. After all, did they not live in the highest branches of the tallest trees? Or on the sacred rocks just off the coast, or in the silent meadows and lagoons where the sun lay down its face to sleep? And did they not give birth to their children year after year? Did they not cry and sing in the early morning in order to wake up the Forest Mother?

The Forest Mother was invisible, but the villagers with the names of birds could feel her presence. They believed she guarded the humans who lived in the village, the humans who carried the names of the flying spirits called birds. They believed she helped the crops grow and the air breathe.

Now there were two special children in the village, a boy named Nuthatch, and a girl named Finch. They were special because they were kind to each other, because they loved to sing, and because they could see the Forest Mother.

The Forest Mother chose them because she loved their singing. Their voices were sweet and their laughter moved the sun on the leaves. They were gentle like the forest birds, like the wind in the pines and eucalyptus trees at dusk.

Forest Mother brought visions to Nuthatch and Finch because she loved them, and the children told their visions to the elders, who listened patiently and carefully to all they described; nodding their greying heads as if to say, yes it is so.

One of the visions sent by Forest Mother saved the village, for she warned them of a high tide and terrible storm that was to wash away their homes. Nuthatch and Finch saw this storm in their Mind's Eye, and they saw all the villagers retreating into the forest until it was over.

So the villagers took refuge with the forest, waiting in the farthest glen until the storm passed. When it was over, they returned to the village to rebuild their fires and gather their lives together again. Everyone returned except for Nuthatch and Finch. They chose to stay in the forest. They lived there a long, long time. Happily too! They lived in the trees like their namesakes. The trees loved them and the birds enjoyed their company, teaching them many new songs. And always the Forest Mother guarded them.

All was well until the morning the terrible noise began. It

76

was a far away noise of whining and grinding. Nuthatch and Finch had never heard such a sound, and it disturbed them. Day after day the noise grew closer and louder until Nuthatch and Finch went to search for the source of such a trial, to see what might be the cause of such ear splitting furor.

It did not take long to find the large men with chain saws, with yellow trucks and cranes and tractors, who were cutting down the Forest Mother's trees, one by one, and very quickly.

Nuthatch and Finch ran back to warn the villagers, and when they heard these things, all the men and women gathered in front of the trees, telling the men with machines to go home, to leave the giant trees alone.

"They belong to the Forest Mother," they said. "You must not take away these trees. They are home for the birds and home for our children Nuthatch and Finch. Look up and you will see they have their homes in the topmost branches."

"These trees do not belong to the village and there is no Forest Mother," laughed the biggest man with the biggest chain saw. "Now out of the way. I have orders from the boss, who is the King of Everything, the KOE we call him. It is he who owns this forest, and we are here to cut trees for building wood and toilet paper." So the biggest man, with the biggest chain saw, pushed the villagers out of his way. and pulled the chain on his saw. But Nuthatch and Finch had run back to their home in the tallest red-wood, and when the biggest man with the biggest chain saw spied them high, high in the top of the tree, he called them to come down.

"COME DOWN OR WE WILL CUT YOU DOWN," he shouted, spitting on the ground and wiping the back of his hand across his mouth. "You will come down. You will obey us. I am the biggest man with the biggest chain saw, and you must do what I say."

"You'd best go down, Finch," said Nuthatch. "I don't want you to be hurt. I am going to stay here with the birds who are our friends, even if they cut this tree down."

"No, my friend. If you stay, so will I. We will stay together, and if they cut us down, we will fall together, like birds who have grown too old to live," Finch replied.

"But we are young, too young to die, and you are too kind to fall to earth like a wingless bird."

"I will not leave this tree without you. I will never leave you, my friend."

Then the Forest Mother whispered to them. "Go, my children, you are too beautiful to die. It is better you live to tell the story of the man with the biggest chain saw. But give him a chance to change his mind. Ask him once more to put down his saw and leave this tree to stand."

So Nuthatch and Finch began the decent. From the ground they looked like tiny brown spiders, clinging to the sweet bark of the giant redwood. When they reached the ground, the biggest man with the biggest chain saw stepped up to them, towering over them like an oppressive smell. "Now you will wear these handcuffs," he laughed. "Now you will go to jail. You are trespassing on the property of the King of Everything. the KOE himself! And because you were so slow to obey, you will now watch the giant tree be brought to earth. Perhaps it is something you need to see." Once more the biggest man spat on the ground.

The village gasped to hear such malevolence. They were horrified to see the look of satisfaction that crossed over the biggest man's face, and they realized then, that some ancient evil had risen from the earth and possessed the mind of the biggest man with the biggest saw. And they knew it would take a village to defeat such a man.

Finch and Nuthatch wept when the chain saw bit into the flesh of red wood.The tears covered their faces and the village wept too.

"Stop," pleaded Finch. "This land belongs to Forest Mother, not the King of Everything. She is begging you to leave the rest of her forest in peace."

But the biggest man with the biggest chain saw did not stop. He sneered and cut until at last the tree was brought low. When it fell to the ground, and lay flat on its side, it still towered above the biggest man. But the biggest man did not even look at it. He turned and tipped back his hard hat. "Now maybe you will listen the next time I speak."

"It is you who should listen to us," said Finch. "Even lying on her side, this red wood tree is taller than you, biggest man. Your heart is blackened, and you will never find happiness."

Nuthatch and Finch were taken away to the town owned by the King of Everything. The name of the town was Mall Town, and they were put in the Mall Town Jail. They huddled together waiting to see if the villagers could get them released. They wanted to return to the village by the sea, for Mall Town was a sickening place to these Lost Forest Children.

The villagers waited outside the jail, chanting, "Let them go, let them go, let our lost forest children come home. Nuthatch and Finch," they shouted. "Nuthatch and Finch. The King is a thief. The King is a thief." Over and over they chanted and sang.

Now the KOE did not like to hear himself bandied about in public. He was a sneaky little king, and he sent the Big Men with the Big Saws out to do his dirty work.

"Send them home now. Martyrs make bad press," said the KOE. Maybe now they have learned about the laws of ownership and possession."

The Lost Forest children returned with the villagers to the edge of the sea. The villagers told their story for many years, so that children would understand what bravery is.

The Biggest Man with the Biggest Chain Saw went on working for the KOE, and when he got older and overweight, he died of a heart attack. But the KOE had a stable full of biggest men, and chose another to do his work.

Now, the Forest Mother roamed like a ghost through the nightsleeps of the KOE, allowing him no rest, bringing wringing wrenching nightmares to the King, who woke screaming after dreaming about falling redwoods crushing him. He fired the current Biggest Man, and took away his chain saw. The biggest man couldn't find another job, and went hungry in his old age like the rest of the stable full of big men owned by the King of Everything. The King of Everything never stopped having bad dreams or firing the biggest men. His mind was ever after filled with sawdust, and he forgot everything, muttering to himself, "'You seen one redwood, you seen 'em all.' Now who was it always used to say that?" He drank copiously of bad spirits, as befitted a man of his particular rank.

The forest mother made new trees grow, and covered the village with sunshine. Nuthatch and Finch never did learn to obey, but they grew up and married and had many children who loved the forest. My grandmother was one of them, and as I told you, her brothers were loggers, and she was a storyteller.

I Came Home
That Morning

Sharon Sue Savage

SHARON SUE SAVAGE

Sharon Sue Savage, born and christened at the end of the depression, was raised in a small town in northern Indiana. Her parents were both teachers, owning a small farm and dairy as supplemental income to their meager salaries. The eldest of four children, she was responsible for much of the upbringing of her younger siblings. Growing up during World War II, she learned early how to be thrifty, to make use of all resources, to raise and preserve your own food, and make your own clothing,

She attended the same school all twelve years and the local Methodist Church. Married in an Ethical Culture ceremony in New York, part of the beat generation, she and her first husband moved to San Francisco. She fed the 'flower children' in the Panhandle of Golden Gate Park. Later she and her husband traveled in Europe for a year, living in a van with three small children, conceiving a fourth on the beach in Valencia.

When she returned with her family to San Francisco, she became actively involved in an art program in the San Francisco public schools, co-authoring The Alvarado Experience, a book about school-community art projects.

She and her second husband spent many years camping in remote areas of the Western United States, settling on thirty acres in the Bitterroot Valley in Montana, where she lived for six years.

Ms Savage says about her writing, *"My grandmother kept a diary, writing something every day. When I was ten, she gave me a diary and I have been writing ever since. Writing for me is at times an escape and at times exciting. It is always healing. I am most inspired to write when I am in contact with nature. Flowers, sunsets, water in motion, the moon in a dark sky move me to try to convey in words what I see and feel. Sometimes, when I dance, poetry just comes."*

IN REFLECTION

In my garden,
a reflecting pool
that has no bottom

thousands of leaves
rest on its smooth as glass surface,
shades of green float, catch

sunlight,

florescent, chartreuse
behind gnarled and twisted
black limbs of a towering oak

wind blows
branches sway
leaves flutter
colors change,

irridescent, opalescent
images distort
like a crystal ball

the deeper you look
the more appears

a body floats
below the surface
hands dripping blood

still alive

pulsating lips
ear lobes, labia
finger tips touch
caress

deeper still,
the sun is surrounded
with a phantom purple corona,

only in the pool
only in the depths
only in reflection

the sky is clear

SHARON'S JOURNAL

"I am amazed daily by the wonderment of life, the syncronicity of events, my connection to it all. Although each of us seems so small and insignificant, we are an integral part of the whole. This week has been a revelation. Each step I've taken, each thing I have done, has shown me things I needed to see, has pointed me in the direction of my path. It looms larger each day. I am writing my story as I live day by day, feeding the animals, covering the rose bushes for winter, doing the work that needs to be done in the garden, cooking some special food and watching the sun and moon rise and set. I am again feeling my place in the universe."

SPRING STORM

Dark clouds
bright sky
shadow shapes shift,

light shafts
pierce the mountains' edge.
Rain comes.

I CAME HOME THAT MORNING

I came home that morning, the morning you ended your life, not knowing that *our life together* was over. As I drove down the lane I looked at the barn door to see if it was open the same way. I have been doing that every day since last November when I found you in the barn, cold and shaking with the shot gun propped on the floor, pointed at your face.

For the last few days when I came home in the evening and there were no lights on in the house, I felt panic. Then I would see you get up and turn a light on and I would breathe a sigh of relief. The premonitions have been with me but I immediately dismissed them as soon as I saw you were there, safe in the house.

To myself I whispered, "Don't make something happen by thinking about it." But the dread was there. I was feeling it in the pit of my stomach.

That morning though, as I looked toward the barn, I saw the door was closed, the three dogs jumping and whining, trying to get in. I knew. I did not want to know, but I knew.

"No!" I yelled, jumping out of the truck. "I will not go out there and look in that barn."

Instead I came in the house and felt immense relief when I saw your shoes sitting under the table. I even felt a little foolish that I had jumped to the conclusion that you were in the barn because the dogs were at the door. They had now run up to the house, jumping and barking.

When I came around the corner and saw the empty bed, my stomach catapulted to my toes, then up to my throat.

I ran out in the yard yelling, "Bill! Bill! Answer me, Bill! Are you there? I am not going to come in that barn for you again! You come out of there right now! If you're in there come out! Please, please come out. Please, Bill, please."

I came back in the house and called my friend Nancy to come over to go with me to look in the barn but there was no answer. I tried my neighbor Charlie but got his answering machine. I left a message for him to come over if he was there and just not answering the phone. I could think of no one else to call. I didn't want to call the sheriff or 911 because I didn't know if it was necessary. I had to go into the barn.

The dogs were back at the barn door barking and jumping up on it. I opened the door a crack and peered in. I saw you sitting there, leaning back against the bales of hay, and I swear your eyes were open. Again I felt instant relief. Then terrible anger. It was both light and dark in the barn. You were so still and peaceful, the gun in your hand, a small trickle of blood running down your chest. The dogs were at you, on you, licking you, licking the blood.

I yelled, "Get up, Bill. Stop playing these games."

I walked over and kicked you. I stumbled over you to get to the other side of you where there was more light so I could see if you were breathing. It was so dark in the barn. I couldn't see anything. I couldn't breathe.

Then the nurse took over. She left the wife, the lover, the friend and became the uninvolved observer. Lift the wrist. Check for a pulse. None. Check respirations. None. Call the police. Do I need an ambulance? No! Shaking so hard I can barely look up the phone number but don't call 911. Call the police. Call forwarded to the sheriff's office. They will be here in fifteen minutes. What do I do now? Maybe I made a mistake. Maybe there was a pulse. Maybe I should go check again. Maybe I should do CPR. No! I know he is dead. I do not want to go back in the barn.

I call Bob, Bill's shrink, at home. Unbelievably he answers the phone. Numbly I say, "Bill just killed himself. I need you to come be with me. I don't know what to do."

"I'll be right over," he replies, and hangs up.

I look out the window at the mountains in the blinding sunlight. I go out in the yard and scream and yell. I am throwing shovels full of manure on the flowerbeds.

"You will not do this to me. I will not let this get me down." I am crying and screaming. Or am I sitting silently in the house, waiting? It feels like eternity has passed and I have probably been home from work no more than ten minutes. Bob arrives and a few minutes later the sheriff.

Now the dogs are barking ferociously. The old dog has always hated uniformed men. I had closed the barn door to keep the dogs out of there but there is no way they are going to let a uniformed man into that barn. Now I feel like a robot. I am operating on automatic pilot only but I do not want the dogs to bite the sheriff. They won't come away from the barn door. I come into the house and get sausage to coax them away, and finally get the young dogs, two year old Alaska Huskies, tied up, and the old dog into the the sceened back porch.

I sit at the picnic table with Bob while the sheriff goes into the barn to do what ever he does, determine death, time, cause. But what he can not do, is determine reason. That is the question that remains unanswered.

Now three years have passed. I go back to the barn. I have been in the barn many times but I have not really looked at it. I have done nothing in the barn since that day. It is exactly the same. I have to go inside and look at this terror that awaits me. It is there, sitting in the barn. It is you, dead, that I do not want to face, that I do not want to confront. It is knowing that I am alone and not knowing how to go on without you.

I am in the barn screaming. I am screaming so loud that it almost breaks my eardrums. I am screaming my anger, my agony, my fear, my terror. The screams are welling up in my throat and choking me. I fall down on top of you. I beat you with my fists until I am heaving up my guts. I want to kill you. I want to hurt you like you hurt me. I want you to know how it feels to be left behind, alone without the one you love. I love you so much. I love you more than life. I once told you that and now I must choose. Without you, without our love, I feel no life. You have taken your life, and with it our love and my dream. But you cannot take my life. I will continue to live.

On that morning when I came home and found you, I shut myself off to saying good bye. I wanted to cradle your big lion head in my arms. I wanted to lie on top of you and never let you go. I wanted to pull you inside of me, to feel you against me, to wrap your dead arms around me. I wanted to cover your face with kisses, your eyelids the way you loved it, telling me how tender my lips were. I wanted to kiss those full sweet lips, from which so many words continuously poured. I wanted to lick away the blood and make it all right again. But I did none of these things.

So today, I am moving. I have sold this place where we came together. I am leaving the ghosts. It is time to say good bye. I kneel down and light sage beside the bale of hay. I whisper to your spirit.

"Be free, my love, be free."

I walk out and close the barn door.

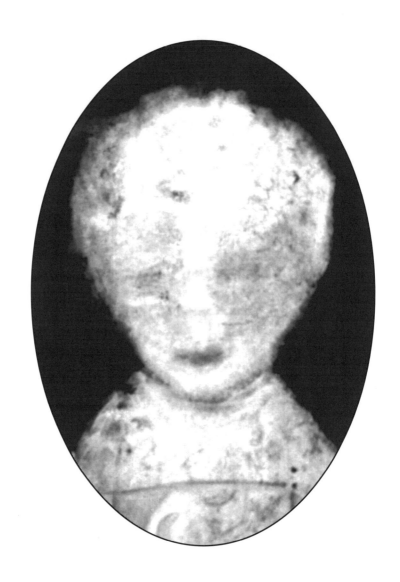

Give Them This
CB Follett

CB FOLLETT

CB Follett has been nominated for five Pushcart prizes and is the author of The Latitudes of Their Going, Gathering the Mountains (Hot Pepper Press, 1993 and 1995) and Visible Bones (Plain View Press, 1998). In 1996 she started a small independent publishing company, ARCTOS PRESS, which has published two anthologies: Beside the Sleeping Maiden, Poets of Marin (1997) and GRRRRR, A Collection of Poems about BEARS (2000). She is also an artist, working in acrylic mixed media.

Speaking about her work, she says, *"In many ways, the two art forms interact with each other. The eye of the painter is good for the poet and visa versa, and many of my paintings include words, phrases, sometimes entire poems. A child of New England, I grew up along Revolutionary roads, splashed in rivers with complicated Indian names, sailed small boats over a salty Sound, skated on ponds named for unknown people, and fell in love with words and the outdoors. As early as I can remember I wrote stories. Poems came later, after I'd passed the half-century mark.*

"Outdoors we ran through the woods playing war games, learned the silhouettes for Messerschmitts and Zeros, worried during blackouts and 'duck and cover'. Every week I walked my Welsh terrier to the library and took out as many books as I could carry. At least two, by maternal decree, had to be "good books" which I presumed to mean classics. I wolfed down every sort of book, reading on the porch glider, in the crook of our chestnut tree, on the living room couch, sprawled on my bed, and later at night, hidden under my covers with the flashlight. Until college, I always assumed I would be a writer, but as so often happens, I ran into a professor so mean-spirited and discouraging that I didn't dare take my own writing seriously.

"When we moved to Sausalito, I grew bold and took the plunge, chasing 'my' great American novel, but instead discovered poetry, which cast itself into me, gave a vigorous shake and set the hook. After years of hunger, I was ravenous.

IF YOU SAW ME

If you saw me
walking some distance ahead,
if you knew my shape
as you used to know it with your hands,
if you saw my shape back-lit against the water,
if you saw the water as it rose and fell
against the shore, saw the lace it tatted like a shawl
around my feet, would you
call out, ask the wave
to tighten its frothy hold?
Would you hold me there,
a small oval in your eye,
far away, the wave receding,
loosening its silk from my ankle?
Would you quicken your pace
or would we stay two
along a stretch of sand, keeping
the distance between us
regularly measured?

If you saw me,
if your eyes said woman
if your mind said her,
would your heart tilt forward or shrink back?
What can we still do to each other,
isolated from our past
yet dragging it with us like seaweed
whipped around our legs, caught
in the sand like the metal camel-hobbles,
the ones we made our guests
try to identify, the intricate interlockings,
flaps to keep sand out of places
that must turn in order to hold? Did sand
get in the locks of our hearts?
Do you think any of this as you watch
the island that is me, dark
against the spangle of ocean, like
Lot's Wife looking back
along this beach we knew so well.

GIVE THEM THIS

Look, I've told you before about hips,
about the early goddess statues
that celebrate curves and rounding flesh:
prosperity, fertility, lust.

Ah Lust

Give them something to run their hands
down, I say. Give them a pawful, a palmful,
something to wrap their fingers around.

Give them melon flesh and musk scent.
Give them skin soft as watercolor
and feet like the petals of magnolia.

Give them river-hands and tumulus of belly
so the hand slides without a hitch of bone.
It's not rib and hip joint they want to stroke,

not reef or rockbound coast.
They want ocean.
They want land that yields.

They want to feel
they've gotten hold of something:
give them mountains.

Let them climb hand over hand
across the foothills
from base camp to base camp.

Let them reach the top, the apex,
the acme of the world, and without rest
start down the other side.

Keep them traveling the continents.
Let them taste the inlets, the outcrops.
Let them tongue salt and cinnamon.

Let them lap it, and lip it,
and enter, and divide, and explode,
and submit:

and now,
and now if we are willing,
let them rest.

I DRINK WATER IN HER NAME
(Greek idiom)

I lift the glass, water
pure from the spring, raise it
toward you, my friend, my moth,
my woman of the ear.

You, who come in smiling,
climb to my upper floor and nestle there
in blue chairs where we pour the waters
of our minds out in cool rivers.

Water that braids into rapids
carrying us with the flow of our words.
We wade, we push off, we swim together,
these are my words, these yours.

They meet, twine and the river slides us
over rocks into calm pools on the still side
of granite. We have been here before. Our river
cascades through storm and downpour,

but as it runs, as we take on water shapes
and liquid in our tongues, we can speak
without sound. Those months I don't see you,
thoughts store in the silo of my mind.

They rustle like corn, scratch like wheat,
compact and push down, waiting.
When you call and say you are near,
I set aside time and stir the silo's crop,

jostle it into lightness so that when you come,
from this dry farmland where I have been restless,
the river sound is heard in the distance, rushing
and crashing to get at us, to sweep us away

in its fine free-fall. The silvers and blues
are like patchwork and from the shore
we slip from our covering and plunge into the midst
of its run: no kicks, no strokes, no struggle,

only surrender to its speed, its volume, the sibilance
of its rush. It closes over us. We are water sprites
again, nereids, naiads, scales flashing.
To you, my friend: I drink water in your name.

PUSHING TOWARD LIGHT

In the dark, red-lined chamber,
warm, safe, where the weight-bearing bones
swim in fluid like the arms of galaxies
and the head is cradled, the legs, the heart
is cradled, where the ocean rocks the shore
and the little boat that is the body
sleeps and wakes in easy stages, and the music
of the spheres is woodwinds and drumbeats.

What then wakes the body to air,
the push against resistance
until only one channel is left to be tried
and the being starts the long/short journey
not yet knowing the crash of light at the end
the manipulation of hands
and the cold measures of metal.

This insistence toward air.
The slippery hard-working transfer from
one element to the next. How we begin by swimming
how water holds and comforts us
how we can float secure on the safe tether
until some signal, when the cradle becomes the cage
and the desperate unknown need to breathe
sends us streamlined, tight-fitted, down the chute.

No one stays behind. Gravity
takes our rubbery arms and pulls us like a cork
from the bottle. The air rushes at us, and the sun.
The sure fingers of our tribe gather us in.
From now on, we are people of the air.

ON THE SIXTH DAY

She took a pinch of clay from the mouths of rivers
where they gather before their last race to the sea:
from the Ebon, thick as oil, rich with loam
carried from forests where leaves overlap
and light comes in small celebrated angles,

and from the Négro, rich earth of cropland,
soil pulled from the embrace of roots,
from tubers and taros, from the supporting of stalks
and pods, from the sprawl of squash and gourd,
from the nightshade's globed lanterns,

and she took from the Rouge,
rummy with the blood of bison and salmon,
of wolves still free
to throw their songs against the wind,
red of the wild roans with delicate hooves,
red of fire and spark,
red of heartline and mesa.

From the Huang, river of light, where sparrows
spin their dialects of song over meadows
tipsy with flowers, and for her last,
she reached cold to the north,
running white with ice where little is seen
but tracks and the brushed blur of a wing
and the firs are like green candles
against the long nights.

From each she scooped clay and fashioned
the five great tribes, woman and man,
and into each pair mixed soil from the others
so they could never be entirely
what they thought they were,
and into each set of ears, she whispered
different stories from the same myth.

RIVER BANKS

River has a silver string that runs its length,
holds it to a source in the mountains.
River cradles its corded muscles of water
between high banks, giving the banks no thought

as it bites them with eddies,
eroding their lower flanks.
River thinks it is only water and the gristle
of currents, haystacking surfaces

and deep, bellowing falls
running for the sea, though
it does not know it is there.
River should take more care of its banks.

Banks are what hold it a river, give
direction, keep it mitering downward.
Without banks, river loses its way,
becomes a swamp and stills.

All my life I have chafed at river banks,
fighting to spread my currents
in whatever turn needed exploring.
The high song of freedom seemed

to be a music of 'no banks',
and yet the whole joy of rivers is pushing,
etching the banks to join the flow,
but having them hold.

SOMETIMES I REMEMBER WINGS

Once I had wings, pale against the high coast of sun.
They grew from my small body
floating in the rich sea of earliest life, wings
I kept folded because the space was snug
and grew tighter as I swam my way toward air.

Thick muscles held them to bones
giving the breath of promise
for wings are made for air
and air was the light I traveled toward.

After the push and the hot wet tunnel, I remembered
my wings, that they should open now,
that they should lift my body above the struggle
of gravity and carry me into the arms of wind.

They remained closed.
I could feel the strong bridge from scapula
to shaft, could feel them tense against the resistance
that comes with earth. Feathers stirred,
brushing my skin but the wings
remained furled as a scroll.

I bore their weight with hope but finally
began to forget, learned to depend
on feet and the unyielding soil
to keep me upright and wings
became only a small point of envy
awakened by birds.

NOT ONE OF THOSE GIRLS

I'm not one of those girls you'd call Babe
or dare to lay on your sweet talk,

not one of those girls who thinks the word
lady connotes anything I ever wanted to be,
who thinks cucumber sandwiches with their
crusts cut off are part of the basic food groups
and I'm not one to let him get away with talking
about the men and girls at his office,

and yet, girl is what I am after all
with my feet bare and clothes not quite matching,
girl with a good pocket in my fielder's mitt,
girl of trees and ice castles, of an inside curve
and still the girl who wore her first strapless gown
like an erector set with the little bolts missing
from strategic connections.

I'm not one of those girls who *lunch,*
and bid game while discussing recipes,
not one who settles for the doctor's
there there dear, don't you worry about it,

but I'm still a girl who's about thirty years
younger than I've aged to,
who carries the eight-year old and sixteen
and twenty-seven-year old as friends of the heart,
and I'm one of those girls whose bones creak,

who begins to acknowledge the fine hand of time
that jerks the body around to remind us
no matter how much we remain one of those girls,
parts of us need more oil than they used to.
I was not one of those girls who listened
to her mother, but snuck out and walked
in the cool breeze of midnight
along roads ending in country,
wind stirring the scent of newly opened maple,

and I'm still the girl who got scared of distance
and shadow but kept walking,
and when I got home, I was the girl
who listened to the wringing of my mother's hands
and knew I would go again.

Wings of Another Era

Doreen Stock

DOREEN STOCK

Doreen Stock is author of <u>The Politics of Splendor</u>, (Alcatraz Editions, 1985). She has published other writers, organized poetry readings, kept poetry alive for others, and continues to publish poems of depth and unique content. Always she brings us back to ourselves, by showing us a 'language of the exquisite'. Here is what she says about heself and her work:

"I am a poet, literary translator, and prose writer. My favorite poem continues to be "The Song of Songs". A verse of this poem from the Old Testament was sung at the artifact of my wedding. Thirty-seven years later, I am amazed at the truths I continue to unearth in this beautiful text, which reveals a profound separation between the lover and the realized woman. ("Architecture and Ecstacy: A Reading of the Song of Songs", published Spring, 2000, in <u>Kerem</u>*).*

Reading old and writing new, this is the core of my aesthetic, along with attention to my dreams and the daily news. Also, I am fortunate to have travelled widely in Europe and the Middle East during the past seven years.

Wings of Another Era was composed on my return to Mill Valley, CA, where I am currently living, writing, and studying."

WINGS OF ANOTHER ERA

I. Flight

Into the waning months
toward the millennium
Into the flat corridors
of silent cloud
the jet stream
heavy with cargo

Our giant wings
flop and rattle
We bend over
small dinners
red wine rolling
down the aisles

and white; champagne
in small bottles

while two faces bend
toward each other

is it Hugh Grant?
is it Julia Roberts?

a child's hand is sliced
by barbed wire at the UN
compound in East Timor

another face, that of a baby,
surfaces from the rubble
of the earthquake in Taiwan

the horrid wars mix with the grinding
of the earth's plates as, flame-like,
a wing from another era moves
into the night side of the earth

crumpled, wet, as if newborn,
crumbling around the edges
as if ancient stone-carved
and veined

with the pale tragedies
that sing into the dark
wind always at our backs

lips from another era press
into mine from behind my face

to write from the lips of others

is considered a sacred act
in any age

Silently, steadily, yellow candles
burn down and we guide our planeloads
toward the airport.

If they would stop trying
to sleep through the flight
they would feel us everywhere
rising over tears and honor, screams
and the stopping of a single breath

coloring the tips of our feathers

gold.

II. Bodies

There are hollows
in my body
that will never
be filled

Places where you have
grazed with small pearls of
teeth as they once surfaced in
my hand at the dig at Ein Gedi

Small pearl teeth
set into a palate
of dusty ivory

I have seen you moving over me
soft black fur sprouting like

delicate moss touching your flesh
curling around it. Each hair on your
body lifting it into a breeze that
surrounded you.

To be touched again by that breeze
I would need to fly back
toward you, the centuries
falling away.

Ah, your knee, only that
rising in marble

Ah, your throat,
only that, in granite

Only your belly in onyx,
only your shoulder, the right
one in chalk.

Were all of this to crumble,
the dust of it would not fill
the spaces
where you have touched me
and fled.

Fleeing becomes you.

Then your black hair streams back
from your brow and your lax
palm confronts the next century
fingertips not reaching out
but curling elegantly
beckoning no one.

III. Poem for an August Bride
for Sana James

On a clear dark night
in years to come
perhaps I will look
out onto the San Francisco Bay.

A boat will come
into being, a Ferry
as in all important moments,
there's a Ferry!
The Greeks knew of this,
cloaked their endings in dark
waves with a light
known only to them.

A beginning is when
the boat turns suddenly, the
light the same, the waves the
same, but jewelry spills out
from every shore into time.

We mark such beginnings
with laughter.

IV. For Anne, Cycling in Virginia
In memory of Anne Neeley

I always imagined
that green leaves
were a little greener

for you

and somehow all of that
speed and light went into
your personal window
of exhilaration to create

a super technicolor world!

Your words were like that;
warm and spiced with intense
feeling...

When we cannot ask more time,
depth is the bottom line, Anne,
I remember you diving off a
high bridge into a small deep pool
at the Trinity River one summer

Goddesses of the ancient world were
born that way, coming up out of the
green water with their lips parted,
tossing diamonds out of their short
sculpted hair

Born to challenge us, the flame buried
behind their faces, a flame whose meaning
we are left to discover as we stare
at their gorgeous enigmatic presences
surfacing broken from the rubble of ages

Dust to dust, yes, but out of dust
these holy faces of the feminine are pushed
forward to reveal us to ourselves

When you woke into your greenest morning
pushed your silver wheels toward it
and were slammed into the planet in new way
I like to think
that you rose to the challenge as always, and,
instead of stopping, you sped into the elements
so that now as I sit before this green tree,
this blue sky, this small toast-colored road,
I think Anne, Anne, Anne.

V. The Face at Zippori
for Tina Chase

1.

The emblem of this ancient city
a beautiful Roman woman
fixes us with her brown gaze,
one eyebrow lifted slightly over
a few mosaics flown off into the
ages exposing the hard-packed
Galilee cement onto which she was
composed.

Designed in earthtones as you are,
her brown hair is elegantly coifed,
and, falling from each ear, an earring
of coral, white, and gold.

She addresses me full face as you do
a small replica of Eros standing
on her right shoulder his bow pulled taut.

How often we have spoken of him in
some guise or another, husband, lover,
son.

And out of the surrounding hunt, of
birds and beasts imbedded in the black
chips of an ancient sky, she tells me,
as you often do, that these moments can
be shot with light instead of arrows,
and that the hunt can become a sacred
dance.

The artisans of Zippori set a wreath of
laurel leaves into her braids and twists
 of hair. Each leaf can be brushed with
water to shine again, that
we read them, and slowly come to see
what she lived, what we live.

2.

If she lived, she came, perhaps, in a time
of conquest to this high plateau overlooking
four valleys. Did her husband wash his blood-
stained hands in this cold spring water? The
graves surround Zippori in the farthest
perimeters. Was she familiar with them?
Did she go there in the end, or back to Rome?

I like to imagine that we were friends then,
too, a friendship leaping all barriers as I
walked one day up from the neighboring Jewish
quarter. Perhaps we met in a flash of recognition
in the narrow streets of Zippori as we once did
in a public park. If someone had told me then,"you

are about to meet an eternal friend," would
I have stopped pushing my child on the swing for
an instant and recorded your face, the leaves
of the bay laurel tree pressing against your
20th century brow with flickerings of light?

3.

As I stand on scaffolding around the living room
floor in which she is imbedded, I imagine you and
I here. I've just come in parched from the heat and
we are sitting on pillows and drinking chilled wine.
The mosaic on your living room floor teaches
us of the God Dionysos, and shows the horrors of
drunkenness. Herakles is sloppy drunk on
your stone carpet!

Did we slyly laugh at this? Or were we too
repressed?

The winds of this place are hot and dry in June. A
bird sounds as it must have sounded while we tried
to share our hearts in the hot silence. Were there
servants listening? Was I, a Jew, even allowed into
the mansion?

Or perhaps I came here merely to deliver something to you. A piece of woven work, or a bit of
pottery or glass.

Was there again, as these objects passed from my
hand to yours, that flicker of eternal recognition?
My friend, my star, my time...

June l999, Jerusalem

115

VI. Chorus of the Butterflies

They live slim, fiery lives
and yet from their vantage

see time deeply.

Once I held, in a dream, the little
shirt you wore to your Uncle's wedding

Sky-blue polished cotton it was
and printed with yellow butterflies

Instantly they surrounded me
and in soft voices cried
out, Oh, that was his? It
looks like him.

I want you to save this, my son.

To be remembered
by the butterflies
is a great compliment.
It means you have been living
your time, deeply.

VII. On Leaving Babies for Eternity
*for the passengers
on Egypt Air Flight # 990*

I've done this.
The last time
it was a two year old

strapped into her car seat
wearing a purple shirt with
the blue denim jumper I brought her
from America, her hair
done up in a curly brown ponytail.

I pulled my luggage from the car
trunk and a quick, stricken look
passed between us. Babies know.

Their mothers don't seem to. Burdened with
milk and grocery lists and a three month old
waiting at home, blue eyes beaming out
of her face, her bare arms chubby in a sprigged
cotton dress the color of clouds and sky,
the threads pulling smocking across her tiny
heart.

She learned to kiss me on the cheek when I was
there. I would bring my face down to hers as she
sat on the table in her infant seat. Mmm! I would
say. And her lips would press against my cheek.
She always smiled afterward. Now they have lit
screens on the airliners. An arrow and a dotted line
with a little airplane on the end of it measures the
heartstring as it pulls across continents, seas, and
rivers of ice.

On taking off this time the jumbo jet
skidded to a stop on the runway, its wings
flapping wildly. "This is it," thought my racing
heart...

The three older boys are already at school. They
would be old enough, should we blip off the radar

screen, to understand. Forget the black box.
Although they spend their days
learning to read the words written by holy men
with black ink on parchment, I would climb
with my bare feet out of the depths of seven seas
to tell them in my own words exactly where I went
and when.

November, 1999

VIII. For Matthew, Who Fell into Time
In Memory of Matt Neeley

As you went
you left signs

I remember
the crescent moon
that morning, with
a darkness around its
bottom cusp

as if there were a hand
holding it

not desperately
not clinging at all

but much like a child's,
who, falling asleep with
a beloved object, clutches
it against his cheek.

This first moon

of our new year
took its place
in the morning sky

with your hand around
it, to signify that heaven

and earth had both deepened,
as a shadow on silver,
to receive you.

IX. Red Tide Toward the Millennium

a small child is climbing
out of a sewer pipe
in Bucharest, Rumania

a grandmother is pleading
for her life to be spared
by a soldier in Chechnya

in Sri Lanka the terrorist
does explode his bomb
killing 300

Mass graves are being dug
in Venezuela today
for the flood victims

as the tides reach toward
the solstice moon higher
and higher they have not yet
formed themselves into words

not yet printed themselves
into tomorrow's news

We have counted 2000 years
and still there are
red happenings rising
before us

We cannot even measure.

X. My Death According to Poetry

My death according to Poetry
leaves me with one arm
already among the angels

its wing pointing earthward
in a sweep of the grey clouds
threatening five valleys
with cold water

My death according to
Poetry leaves me with
one hand clutching
the purse I was given
by my mother

in it a sandwich
I have been eating now for years...

The Salmon that swam into that
sandwich suffered its way

onto a singular hook
and was clubbed over the head.

My death according to Poetry
is printed in pages
of red and white checked oilcloth

that crack
in the center
and will never be published.

There are songs I never sang
according to Poetry

But Poetry lies.

ACKNOWLEDGEMENTS: Several of the poems and pieces of fiction have been published previously in a number of small magazines, newspapers or books. We wish to thank and acknowledge the following: _The Butterfly Chronicles, Vol. I - III, The Pacific Sun, The Rock River Times, Prairie Winds, Poets West Literary Journal, Sow's Ear, Where the Enchanted Live, The Broken String,_ (Plain View Press, 1994), _Noe Valley Voice, The Bernal Journal, MALT Magazine, Standing Wave, Experiments in Flight Icarus, Ambit, The MacGuffin, The Barkeater, The Adirondack Review, Radiance: The Magazine for Large Women._

We wish to acknowledge the following quotation found on a New Zealand T-shirt, the words presumably from the Maori dictionary. It describes many women from all cultures, as well as the artists and writers in **TAMBOURINE**.

wahine purota

"women who have the gift of being
outstanding, strong and loving.
who contribute artistic achievement and
creative excellence to influence
the history and future of aotearoa,
giving lead to future generations.
Enhancing and drawing upon
traditional and contemporary maori
values to express their aspirations and
struggles, thus offering solutions for all
women."

You may order additional copies of
TAMBOURINE by writing:
In Between Books, P.O. Box 790,
Sausalito, CA 94966,
phoning (415) 383-8447,
faxing this form to (415) 381-1938,
or e-mailing In Between Books at
butterflytree@outrageous.net

TAMBOURINE is available at
amazon.com or Barnes & Noble
Bookstores, or can be ordered from
any other bookstore.

ORDER FORM

Please send _____ copies of Tambourine to:

name_____
address_____
city_____state_____ zip_____

price is 14.95 per book

number of copies_____ amount enclosed   _____
discount (20%on orders of 5 or more books)   _____
cost for shipping $5.00 for up to 10 books   _____

TOTAL amount enclosed   _____

For more information or if you have questions
email us at butterflytre @outrageous.net